The New York Times

CHANGING PERSPECTIVES

Climate Change

THE NEW YORK TIMES EDITORIAL STAFF

Published in 2019 by New York Times Educational Publishing
in association with The Rosen Publishing Group, Inc.
29 East 21st Street, New York, NY 10010

First Edition

The New York Times
Alex Ward: Editorial Director, Book Development
Brenda Hutchings: Senior Photo Editor/Art Buyer
Phyllis Collazo: Photo Rights/Permissions Editor
Heidi Giovine: Administrative Manager

Rosen Publishing
Jacob R. Steinberg: Director of Content Development
Greg Tucker: Creative Director
Brian Garvey: Art Director

Cataloging-in-Publication Data
Names: New York Times Company.
Title: Climate change / edited by the New York Times editorial staff.
Description: New York : The New York Times Educational Publishing,
2019. | Series: Changing perspectives | Includes bibliographic refer-
ences and index.
Identifiers: ISBN 9781642820751 (pbk.) | ISBN 9781642820072
(library bound) | ISBN 9781642820065 (ebook)
Subjects: LCSH: Climatic changes—Juvenile literature. | Climatic
changes—Effect of human beings on—Juvenile literature. | Climatic
changes—Government policy—Juvenile literature. | Global warming—
Juvenile literature.
Classification: LCC QC981.8.C5 C556 2019 | DDC 363.738'74—dc23

Manufactured in the United States of America

On the cover: Felix Condori, the mayor of Llapallapani, Bolivia, 31,
former fisherman who now has to make money finding construction
jobs because the lake that his village was built on has disappeared.
He is in a boat in the dry lake bed of Lake Poopó, outside Llapallapani, Bolivia; Josh Haner/The New York Times.

Contents

CHAPTER 3

Scientists vs. Skeptics: The 1980s

CHAPTER 4

Do We Have to Take Action? The 1990s

CHAPTER 5

Reality Sinks In: The 2000s

CHAPTER 6

The Consequences: 2010 and Beyond

Introduction

GLOBAL CLIMATE CHANGE is real. It is not new. And it is not fake news.

The New York Times began reporting on climate change in the mid-twentieth century. But the reality of climate change goes back much further. The concept of climate change has existed since the mid-1800s.

The "greenhouse effect" is how Irish physicist John Tyndall described what happens when light passes through Earth's atmosphere and its heat is trapped by gas. Tyndall's studies showed that certain gases such as carbon dioxide absorbed enough heat to affect the planet's climate. That was in 1861. Swedish scientist Svante Arrhenius later calculated that Earth could warm by as much as 6 degrees Celsius (10.8 degrees Fahrenheit) if the amount of carbon dioxide in the atmosphere doubled.

What could cause such a massive increase in carbon dioxide? Manmade industrial technology, large-scale agriculture, and a growing population. Human-built machines consumed enormous quantities of coal and oil. This released increasing amounts of carbon dioxide into the atmosphere. At the same time, people cleared trees from vast areas of land to farm and to expand cities. With fewer trees to absorb the carbon dioxide, more of the gas stayed in the atmosphere. Global warming had started.

By the late 1940s, Arctic glaciers began to melt, and ocean levels rose. Scientists recognized these as early signs of global warming. Evidence gathered in the 1960s confirmed that the amount of carbon dioxide in the atmosphere was rising each year. And so was the average global temperature. The scientific community agreed in the 1980s

A woman collected water from a pit dug in a dry riverbed near Kakuma in the Turkana District in northwest Kenya. Residents of this semi-arid region are experiencing levels of food insecurity as a result of ongoing drought.

that, if left unchecked, environmental disaster was inevitable. Climate experts called for world leaders to work together to reduce carbon emissions to slow down global warming. But within a decade, the destructive effects of global warming were evident. And they were much worse than climate experts predicted.

In 2001, an international panel of scientists declared that more than half of temperature increase over the previous fifty years was likely caused by human activity. Catastrophic environmental damage was unavoidable unless significant changes were made. Severe heat waves, droughts, floods, and tropical storms would occur more often. Ocean water would continue to warm, and Antarctic ice would melt permanently. The effects on plant, animal, and human life could be devastating. Climate scientists agreed that there was no way to prevent global warming. However, by significantly curbing carbon emissions, it could be slowed down. To underscore their concerns, thousands of scientists took the unusual step of becoming activists. They organized the first annual March for Science in 2017.

To climate scientists, global climate change is a fact. To the fossil fuel industry, however, the modifications required to fight climate change are a huge risk to profit margins. Coal, oil, and automobile companies have worked to discredit the idea of human-caused global warming. They have sponsored studies and ad campaigns implying that there is not enough proof human activity can affect the climate. They have lobbied for politicians to roll back regulations restricting carbon emissions. And they have invested heavily in political campaigns that support their interests. Their efforts are effective. Climate change has even been scrubbed from federal websites as though it doesn't exist. But it does. And in the meantime, water sources are drying up, rising sea levels threaten to flood coastal cities, each year is hotter than the next, and carbon dioxide levels keep going up.

Human-caused global climate change is real. It has been real for over 150 years. And unless human activity changes, it will be devastating.

CHAPTER 1

Early Warnings: The 1940s–1960s

Human-caused climate change was not new when it was reported in 1947. Scientists knew human activity could affect the climate a hundred years earlier. However, melting glaciers, rising ocean levels, and warmer days were early indications that the effects of global warming were real. And that was news.

Warming Arctic Climate Melting Glaciers Faster, Raising Ocean Level, Scientist Says

BY GLADWIN HILL | MAY 29, 1947

LOS ANGELES — A mysterious warming of the climate is slowly manifesting itself in the Arctic, engendering a "serious international problem," Dr. Hans Ahlmann, noted Swedish geophysicist, said today.

Dr. Ahlmann, Professor of Geography at the University of Stockholm and director of the Swedish Geographical Institute, discussed the phenomenon, on the basis of personal research over two decades, at a seminar of the Geophysical Institute at the University of California here.

Since 1900, Dr. Ahlmann said, Arctic air temperatures have increased 10 degrees Fahrenheit, an "enormous" rise from a scientific standpoint.

In the same period, ocean waters in the militarily strategic Spitsbergen area have risen 3 to 5 degrees in temperature, and, apparently because of the accelerated melting of glaciers, one to one and one-half millimeters yearly in level, he said.

"We do not even know the reason behind this climatic change in recent years," Dr. Ahlmann added.

If, however, the cause were of global nature, and "if the Antarctic ice regions and the major Greenland ice cap should be reduced at the same rate as the present melting, oceanic surfaces would rise to catastrophic proportions," he said. "Peoples living in lowlands along the shores would be inundated."

The climatic change was not implausible, Dr. Ahlmann suggested, in view of the fact that "we know that the tropics have felt a marked climatic change in the last fifteen or twenty years, especially in the vicinity of West Africa. Many smaller lakes have actually disappeared and larger ones are drying up. Even huge Lake Victoria has dropped seven inches in the past decade."

The Arctic change, the scientist asserted, "is so serious that I hope an international agency can be formed to study conditions on a global basis. That is most urgent."

One effect of the change, he said, has been to improve navigation conditions along the northern rim of Europe, a development of chief interest to Russia.

"In 1910 the navigable season along western Spitsbergen lasted only three months," he said. "Now it lasts eight months. This is of world strategic importance."

Warmer Climate on the Earth May Be Due to More Carbon Dioxide in the Air

BY WALDEMAR KAEMPFFERT | OCT. 28, 1956

THE GENERAL WARMING of the climate that has occurred in the last sixty years has been variously explained. Among the explanations are fluctuations in the amount of energy received from the sun, changes in the amount of volcanic dust in the atmosphere and variations in the average elevation of the continents.

According to a theory which was held half a century ago, variation in the atmosphere's carbon dioxide can account for climatic change. The theory was generally dismissed as inadequate. Dr. Gilbert Plass re-examines it in a paper which he publishes in the American Scientist and in which he summarizes conclusions that he reached after a study made with the support of the Office of Naval Research. To him the carbon dioxide theory stands up, though it may take another century of observation and measurement of temperature to confirm it.

ABUNDANT GASES

In considering the theory, Dr. Plass reminds us that the most abundant gases in the atmosphere are nitrogen and oxygen. There is also a little argon. These cannot absorb much of the heat radiated by the earth after it has been warmed by the sun. If they could, the climate would be far colder than it is today, because the passage of heat to outer space would not be stopped.

Three other gases could check the radiation of heat. These are carbon dioxide (the gas that fizzes in ginger ale), water vapor and ozone. All these are relatively rare.

To explain what happens, Dr. Plass resorts to the familiar greenhouse analogy. The rays of the sun pass through the transparent glass, but the outgoing energy (heat) from the plants in the greenhouse cannot pass through. Heat is trapped in the greenhouse, with the result that it is warmer inside than outside.

The atmosphere acts like the glass of a greenhouse. Solar radiation passes through to the earth readily enough, but the heat radiated by the earth is at least partly held back. That is why the earth's surface is relatively warm. Carbon dioxide, water vapor and ozone all check radiation of heat.

Of the three gases that check radiation, carbon dioxide is especially important even though the atmosphere contains only 0.03 per cent of it by volume. As the amount of carbon dioxide increases, the earth's heat is more effectively trapped, so that the temperature rises.

All this was first brought to the attention of scientists by Tyndall in 1861. In his day the facilities for studying the atmosphere and measuring its temperature were crude. Today they are highly refined. According to Dr. Plass, the latest calculations indicate that if the carbon dioxide content of the earth were doubled the surface temperature would rise 3.6° C. and that if the amount were reduced by half the surface temperature would fall 3.8° C.

STRIKING CHANGES

Such a comparatively small fluctuation seems of no importance. Nevertheless it can bring about striking changes in climate. If the average temperature should fall only a few degrees centigrade, glaciers would cover a large part of the earth's surface. Similarly a rise in the average temperature of only 4° C. would convert the polar regions into tropical deserts and jungles, with tigers roaming about and gaudy parrots squawking in the trees.

Dr. Plass examines the various factors that enter into what is called the "carbon dioxide balance," including the exchange of carbon dioxide between the oceans and the atmosphere. That balance must be preserved. Photosynthesis (the process whereby plants with the aid of sunlight assimilate carbon dioxide to produce sugars and starches) causes a large loss of carbon dioxide, but the balance is restored by processes of respiration and decay of plants and animals.

Despite nature's way of maintaining the balance of gases the amount of carbon dioxide in the atmosphere is being artificially increased as we burn coal, oil and wood for industrial purposes. This was first pointed out by Dr. G. S. Callendar about seven years ago. Dr. Plass develops the implications.

GENERATED BY MAN

Today more carbon dioxide is being generated by man's technological processes than by volcanoes, geysers and hot springs. Every century man is increasing the carbon dioxide content of the atmosphere by 30 per cent—that is, at the rate of 1.1° C. in a century. It may be a chance coincidence that the average temperature of the world since 1900 has risen by about this rate. But the possibility that man had a hand in the rise cannot be ignored.

Whatever the cause of the warming of the earth may be there is no doubt in Dr. Plass' mind that we must reckon with more and more industrially generated carbon dioxide. "In a few centuries," he warns, "the amount of carbon dioxide released into the atmosphere will be so large that it will have a profound effect on our climate."

Even if our coal and oil reserves will be used up in 1,000 years, seventeen times the present amount of carbon dioxide in the atmosphere must be reckoned with. The introduction of nuclear energy will not make much difference. Coal and oil are still plentiful and cheap in many parts of the world, and there is every reason to believe that both will be consumed by industry so long as it pays to do so.

Scientists Agree World Is Colder, But Climate Experts Meeting Here Fail to Agree on Reasons for Change

BY WALTER SULLIVAN | JAN. 30, 1961

AFTER A WEEK of discussions on the causes of climate change, an assembly of specialists from several continents seems to have reached unanimous agreement on only one point; it is getting colder.

As to why there are such changes — either from decade to decade or in terms of the ice ages — no explanation was sufficiently convincing to win majority support. Many schools of thought were represented in the five-day discussions and, while the debate remained good-humored, there was energetic dueling with scientific facts.

The participants had come as far afield as Australia and Hungary to the conference held at the Barbizon Plaza from Tuesday to Saturday. Their techniques ranged from observations with earth satellites to such methods as palynology, dendrochronology, and the deciphering of ancient oriental scripts.

Palynology analyzes pollens, in ancient sediments, to determine what plants were growing at that time. These, in turn, serve as clues to the climate of the period. Dendrochronology makes use of tree-ring spacing to study cyclic weather changes.

THEORIES ARE ADVANCED

These and many other methods have been used to test some of the scores of theories that have been advanced to explain the ice ages. Such periods of glaciation have not occurred at regular intervals. Rather they seem to have come in batches lasting a million years or so at intervals of one or two hundred million years. We are in the midst or at the end of such a batch, which began roughly 1,000,000 years ago — the Pleistocene.

The theories most extensively discussed this last week depended upon celestial mechanics, upon changes in transparency of the atmosphere, upon changes in the sun and upon a cyclic sequence of events centering on the presence or absence of ice in the Arctic Ocean.

Objections were raised to all of them. A number of the participants seemed to have come away with a suspicion that more than one factor was responsible for the long-term and short-term changes. Thus several of the speakers supported a modification of the theory advanced during the period between the two world wars by M. Milankovitch.

That Yugoslav scientist, in two hundred pages of equations and calculations, attempted to explain the climate changes of the past in terms of three variables: the shape, or eccentricity, of the earth's orbit around the sun; the tilt of the earth's axis; and the relationship between the solstices and the dates when the distance between earth and sun are greatest, and least.

CHANGES ARE SLIGHT

Although changes in these elements may have been slight, it is argued that they have been sufficient to tip the climatic scales in high latitudes and produce more snow than can be melted in summer. This is the basic requirement for an ice age.

Another widely supported view at the conference favored a solar origin. To show the sensitivity of climate to changes on the sun, investigators have long sought to find eleven-year cycles on earth similar to the eleven-year sunspot cycle. Several participants in the conference reported such correlations.

Roger Y. Anderson of the University of New Mexico told of work done by investigators of varves. These are layers of sediment, such as those laid down on the bottom of a lake that are sensitive to changes in weather and the seasons. They can be studied much in the same way as tree rings.

An eleven-year periodicity has been found in several studies, he said. Varve sequences that have been analyzed are both from recent centuries and from prehistoric times, as preserved in sediments that have turned to rock. A similar eleven-year pattern in tree rings extending back several centuries was reported by D. Justin Schove of St. David's College in Kent, England.

He told how he had traced sun spot cycles back 300 A. D. by examining references to auroral displays and sun spots in ancient writings. Auroras, or northern lights, are most frequent at sun spot maximums. He has found what he regards as a parallel pattern in tree rings.

CONTRADICTORY REPORT

Reid A. Bryson and John A. Sutton of the University of Wisconsin reported completely contradictory results. In statistical analyses both of varve and tree-ring data they could find no suggestion of an eleven-year cycle.

Another speaker protested that a researcher could squeeze any cycle he wished out of a mass of data, merely by his choice of the mathematical "filter" that he used.

One of the chief concerns of climatologists in recent years has been the possible role of industrial carbon dioxide in changing our climate. As civilization burns up the world's reserves of coal and oil, the combustion discharges great quantities of carbon dioxide into the air.

It is known that this gas has a "greenhouse" effect. That is, it readily permits the passage of warming radiation in the wave-length emitted by the sun, yet inhibits the escape of this heat back into space. Therefore, the more carbon dioxide in the atmosphere, presumably, the warmer the climate.

From radiocarbon analysis of wood from trees of the preindustrial era, it is thought that the carbon-dioxide content of the air has increased. Hence, our smokestacks have been blamed by some for the warming observed during the early decades of this century.

DUST HELD A FACTOR

This encouraged a belief that the ice ages might be laid to dust or changes in the composition of air linked to periods of volcanic eruption. Last week, however, scientists from Sweden and the United States reported that, in the last two decades, the warming trend seems to have been reversed.

A similar finding has been made by Soviet scientists. This would seem to weaken the contention that industrial smoke can alter the climate.

One way in which it has been proposed that the sun can influence the weather is through the effect of ultraviolet light on the upper atmosphere. Rocket and satellite observations indicate that solar eruptions associated with the sun-spot cycle do not substantially change the total energy output of the sun. However, they do bring about radical fluctuation in ultra-violet radiation.

The difficulty, as noted by some of the conference participants, is that ultraviolet light only influences the extremely thin air at the top of the atmosphere. They argue that changes there can no more affect the mighty weather phenomena lower down than a finger trailing in the water can set in motion a deep ocean current.

OCEAN LEVEL LOWERED

One of the most recent ice-age theories is that advanced by Maurice Ewing and William L. Donn of the LaMont Geological Observatory of Columbia University. In their view the ice ages of the last million years have occurred when the Arctic Ocean was free of ice, permitting winds from the north to pick up moisture and lay heavy snows on near-by lands.

When this process lowered ocean levels enough to curtail the flow of warm water into the Arctic, the ocean froze and the ice sheets shriveled until the ocean rose enough to start the cycle again. This theory, too, was opposed by some of the speakers.

Despite the failure of the conferees to agree, it appeared that the answer might be within their reach. As some of them noted, much remains to be done in refining dating methods with radioisotopes and in collecting data from space, from the ocean floor, and from the continents before a convincing case can be made for one of the rival theories.

The conference was sponsored by the American Meteorological Society and the New York Academy of Sciences. Its co-chairmen were Rhodes W. Fairbridge of Columbia University and Charles G. Knudsen of the United States Weather Bureau.

CHAPTER 2

Heating Up: The 1970s

A growing awareness of the damage human activity was causing the environment inspired the environmental movement. That fueled the demand and funding for climate research. Lengthy droughts in Africa, India, and the Ukraine caused devastating food shortages. Carbon dioxide levels in the atmosphere continued to increase.

The Need to Work in Concert Was Clear

BY WALTER SULLIVAN | JUNE 18, 1972

STOCKHOLM — The charges, countercharges and debates were familiar to those who frequent such meetings, but there is new hope that the United Nations Conference on the Human Environment may mark a historic turning point.

For beneath the polemics ran groundswell of unanimity. Most of the final decisions were made without a dissenting vote. It was as though the nations comprising the family of man had become aware, as never before, of the vulnerability of their planet and how essential it is that they work in concert to preserve it.

Not all members of the family were represented. Because the East Germans had been denied full representation, the Russians and their closest allies stayed away. But the decisions made here must now be ratified by the United Nations General Assembly in the fall, and so the Soviet bloc will have its say. The Russians are likely to protest decisions and commitments made without their participation, but they are unlikely, in the end, to stand in the way of a program so universally supported.

These were the major results of the conference:

• Approval of an "action program" involving some 200 recommendations in fields that range from monitoring climate change or oceanic pollution to promoting birth control and the preservation of the world's vanishing diversity of plant and animal species.

• The recommended establishment of administrative machinery to coordinate the worldwide environmental efforts of governments and international agencies, eliminating overlap and encouraging programs to fill the gaps.

• The approval of an Environment Fund to cover that part of the international effort not paid for by specialized agencies and national governments. Pledges made so far suggest that the fund will reach at least $100 million, which has been considered the minimum requirement for the first five years of operation.

• Agreement after intensive negotiation on a declaration of agreed principles. To the end, however, the Chinese continued to object to its call for a halt in nuclear weapons testing.

While the ideological and economic differences that divide the world did not stand in the way of the basic actions, they emerged sharply in the debates — the United States role in Vietnam, South African apartheid, Brazilian plans for a giant dam that Argentina argues will curtail its water resources. Furthermore, with almost the entire "third world" represented, it was evident that the environmental concerns of developing nations are very different from those of others worried about their industrial smog and urban traffic fumes.

Among the issues that lined the third world up against the industrialized nations was a proposal by India and Libya that an international fund or financial institution be set up to provide "seed capital" to help developing countries improve their housing and other aspects of the residential environment. The third world easily pushed through this plan, but the 15 nations voting against it were those in the best financial position to support it.

In one of its numerous actions, the conference endorsed a birth control proposal submitted by Norway. It would have the World Health Organization and other U.N. agencies increase their family-planning assistance to governments "without delay." The W.H.O. is asked to intensify its support for research on human reproduction "so that serious consequences of the population explosion on the human environment can be prevented."

A series of recommendations was aimed at fears that the rapid adoption by farmers of standard crops is perilously weakening the "gene pool" upon which the long-term survival of such crops is dependent. Where single strain or group of strains is used over a wide area, the crops are vulnerable to sudden blights against which they have no defenses. Often it is in wild or exotic strains that the blight-resistant properties are found.

Yet such strains are fast vanishing. Hence the conference has recommended that governments "initiate immediately" emergency programs of exploration and collection of species listed by the Food and Agricultural Organization as particularly imperiled. A global network of national and regional institutes would store seed and otherwise preserve and develop breeds for posterity.

To many conservation groups and other organizations concerned with the environment, who watched from the sidelines — about 300 of them were represented here — the conference was more important for the change in national attitudes that it symbolized than for what it did. Margaret Mead, the anthropologist, invited to address the conference on behalf of the nongovernmental organizations, said:

"This is a revolution in thought fully comparable to the Copernican revolution by which, four centuries ago, men were compelled to revise their whole sense of the earth's place in the cosmos. Today we are challenged to recognize as great a change in our concept of man's place in the biosphere. Our survival in a world that continues to be worth inhabiting depends upon translating this new perception into relevant principles and concrete action."

Climate Changes Endanger World's Food Output

BY HAROLD M. SCHMECK JR. | AUG. 8, 1974

Bad weather this summer and the threat of more of it to come hang ominously over every estimate of the world food situation. It is a threat the world may have to face more often in the years ahead. Many weather scientists expect greater variability in the earth's weather and, consequently, greater risk of local disasters in places where conditions of recent years have become accepted as the norm. Some experts believe that mankind is on the threshold of a new pattern of adverse global climate for which it is ill-prepared. This is another in a series of articles, which will appear from time to time, examining the world food situation.

A RECENT MEETING of climate experts in Bonn, West Germany, produced the unanimous conclusion that the change in global weather patterns poses a severe threat to agriculture that could lead to major crop failures and mass starvation.

Others disagree, but are still concerned over the impact of weather on man's ability to feed the ever-increasing number of human beings.

Whether or not this year's events are harbingers of a major global trend, some of those events are, of themselves, causing concern.

The monsoon rains have been late and scant over agriculturally important regions of India, while Bangladesh has been having floods.

Parts of Europe and the Soviet Union have had problems at both ends of the weather spectrum this year — too hot and dry at some times and places, too wet and cold at others.

There have been similar problems in North America. An American weather expert recently received reports that ice was lingering abnormally on the coasts of Newfoundland and that new evidence showed that the Gulf Stream was fluctuating toward a more southerly course.

In the United States, the world's most important food producer, a severe drought that began last fall in the Southwest has spread northward and eastward, and may have potentially serious effects in the Corn Belt. There have also been reports that spring wheat in the United States has been badly hurt by hot, dry weather.

Earlier this year, there had been hopes of bumper crops in North America and elsewhere. But the weather's adverse impact has trimmed back some of these hopes.

The situation is not all bad, by any means. Canada's prospects are said to be reasonably good, depending on what happens during the next few weeks. Aside from some floods, Australia has had no serious problems, according to experts in the United States. The Soviet Union has predicted a high grain yield, largely on the basis of a good winter wheat crop. But spring wheat, accounting for about 35 per cent of that nation's total wheat crop, may be suffering from persistent high temperatures and strong winds.

It appears that what is happening now and what will happen in the next few weeks in many areas of the world may be crucial for food production this year.

The Department of Agriculture's mid-July world grain outlook called the situation somewhat less favorable than it was a month earlier.

"The June 14 production estimate was 1,000.5 million metric tons," said the department's estimate, "but as of mid-July, the total output is estimated at only 983,8 million metric tons."

SOVIET ESTIMATE RISES

"The most important changes in crop prospects over the past month have been in the U.S.A. and the U.S.S.R.," said the report on wheat and feed grains. "The latest U. S. crop estimate is approximately 22 million tons below mid-June, whereas the U.S.S.R. estimate has been revised upward by about 11 million tons."

All of the signs, both good and bad, are being watched closely by specialists in weather and its effects on agriculture.

In the whole complex equation of food, resources and population, the element that is least controllable and probably least predictable is weather. Yet, weather can spell the difference between abundance and disaster almost anywhere.

This year, experts in weather, climate and agriculture have given much thought to the prospects for the coming years and decades.

The Rockefeller Foundation sponsored a conference on essentially this subject. A unit of the National Academy of Sciences is preparing a major report on climate change. The Environmental Data Service of the National Oceanic and Atmospheric Administration is organizing a special group of experts to keep close watch on global weather as it relates to food production. And a workshop sponsored by the International Federation of Institutes for Advanced Study prepared a detailed report on the impact of climate change on the quality and character of human life.

The summary statement of that report is one of the grimmest forecasts to be made in recent years. Dr. Walter Orr Roberts, one of the nation's foremost experts on climate, believes there is a growing consensus in his field that agrees with the workshop's assessment.

NEW PATTERN EMERGING

"The studies of many scholars of climatic change attest that a new climatic pattern is now emerging," the workshop's summary said. "There is a growing consensus that the change will persist for several decades and that the current food-production systems of man cannot easily adjust. It is also expected that the climate will become more variable than in recent decades."

"We believe that this climatic change poses a threat to the people of the world," the summary continued. "The direction of climate change indicates major crop failures almost certainly within the decade. This, coinciding with a period of almost nonexistent grain reserves, can be ignored only at the risk of great suffering and mass starvation."

Dr. Roberts, who is program chairman of the federation, said that scientists of several nations participated in the workshop. Its conclusions were unanimous.

Although all scientists do not put the matter in such stark terms and many doubt that a clear change in climate is demonstrable, there is widespread agreement on one point: The weather patterns that have prevailed in recent decades are anything but normal when viewed against the history of the past several centuries.

The mean temperature of the northern hemisphere increased steadily from the early nineteen-hundreds through the early nineteen-forties. Since then, it has been on its way downward toward the colder circumstances of the last century. The drop since the nineteen-forties has only been about half a degree, but some scientists believe this is enough to trigger changes that could have important effects on the world's weather and agriculture.

In recent publications, Dr. Reid Bryson of the University of Wisconsin, one of the chief proponents of the view that climate change is overtaking mankind, has cited India as an example of the possible hazards.

Early in this century, severe droughts seemed to hit northern and northwestern India roughly once every three or four years. In more recent decades, the monsoon rains moved northward and the frequency of droughts declined to about once or twice in 20 years. Dr. Bryson and other scientists now believe that the trend is back toward the less favorable conditions of the early nineteen-hundreds.

Meanwhile, the Indian population has greatly increased and demands on the nation's agriculture have risen accordingly.

Apart from that kind of long-range consideration, the situation in India this year is being watched with particular attention because, in the view of several experts, it is potentially serious.

The heavy monsoon rains vital to India's agriculture seem to be at least a month late, according to the latest world summary of the weekly weather and crop bulletin, published by the Departments of Commerce and Agriculture.

7TH YEAR OF DRAUGHT

Dr. Richard Fetch, one of the weather experts involved in producing the bulletin, said the latest data available to them showed that three-

A Tuareg woman at a camp near Niamey, Niger, where tribespeople are affected by drought. (Reproduction of a photograph that appeared in the print version of this article.)

fourths of the total grain-producing area of India was below normal in rainfall this year. Rainfall was normal at this time last year throughout most of the sub-continent.

The sub-Saharan region of Africa, another area of the world ultimately dependent on monsoon rains, is now in its seventh year of drought.

The region is currently experiencing a brief reprieve as the result of a somewhat wetter rainy season than has been the pattern in recent years. Some observers say the rains may even allow modest crops of sorghum and millet to be harvested.

Even so, most experts view the current rains as only a temporary fluctuation. Dr. Bryson and others believe that the sub-Sahara will continue to suffer the effects of a change in weather patterns that is likely to persist. This, like most other aspects of current climate, is subject to considerable debate among specialists.

One important reason that all of the world's weather signs are being watched closely this year is that the world does not have the margin of safety in food grains that it had a few decades ago.

One specialist said that the world's total grain reserves were equal to the approximate difference between a good crop year and a bad one. Thus, it would take only one bad crop year to draw the safety margin in world food down close to the vanishing point.

That is why experts are keeping a close watch on such diverse phenomena as the late monsoon rains over India, hot weather in the Soviet Union east of the Urals and the moisture in the soil of sunbaked Iowa. Now, perhaps more than ever before in man's history, they all tie together.

Indeed, some scientists believe efforts to build up world food reserves ought to be a major international concern.

Although there is no prospect of a food shortage in North America, specialists are keeping a watchful eye on the Southwest, the Plains States and the Corn Belt because the United States is so important to the world's total food supply.

Lyle M. Denny, who helps Dr. Felah to produce the weekly weather and crop bulletin, said a drought began last fall in West Texas and adjoining areas of the Southwest and has since spread northward and eastward. He said ranchers have had to haul water to their cattle in New Mexico, Arizona and Utah.

PROBLEMS IN IOWA

Dr. Louis M. Thompson, associate dean of agriculture at Iowa State University in Ames, said hot, dry weather had reduced Iowa's potential corn and soybean crops by at least 10 per cent. A sophisticated statistical study of temperature, soil moisture and their effects on crops has led Dr. Thompson to a rough rule of thumb relating temperature to crop yield.

According to this rule of thumb, he said in a recent interview, the corn crop will be reduced one bushel an acre for every cumulative 10 degrees that the temperature rises above 90. For example, if the temperature rises to 95 on a given day, he would record that as a five. If it rises to 100 the next day, he would add 10.

By the end of the third week in July, Dr. Thompson said, the cumulative total reached 114 degrees above 90. For both corn and soybeans, this would mean a reduction in yield of about 10 per cent, according to his calculations. But Dr. Thompson sees more potential significance to the number than the effect on this year's crop.

The record, of 114 has not been approached since the drought year of 1954, when the total through July 21 was 96. The record has not been surpassed since the "dust bowl" drought year of 1936, when the cumulative degrees above 90 in Iowa totaled 236 through the first 21 days of July.

Dr. Thompson said records to 1800 show that the agriculturally important region in which he lives has been hit by a severe drought in a cycle that occurs roughly every two decades. The most recent cycles came in the mid-nineteen-thirties and the mid-fifties, according to his figures. And he notes with little complacency that the next drought would be "due" in the midseventies.

Dr. Thompson and those scientists who agree with him think the timing of the current harsh weather in the West may be more than coincidence. But there is sharp disagreement among experts on this point. Some see no evidence of any cyclical 20-year pattern, and no logical or scientific basis for it.

Specialists in the Department of Agriculture, for example, are among those who disagree with Dr. Thompson. They believe that weather is a random variable, obeying no regular cyclic pattern over the years except, of course, the seasons.

Richard C. McArdle, an economist, and climatologist in the Department of Agriculture, doubts the reality of a 20-year cycle and does not think that there will be a global run of bad weather this year or in the near future. The more likely pattern for any year, he believes, is one in which some areas of the world have good weather for crops while other areas do not. This year's pattern is like that, he says.

BENEFITS OF TECHNOLOGY

He and others in the department also argue that modern agricultural technology and irrigation are capable of mitigating the effects of drought in the United States. This, too, is an area of disagreement among experts. Some doubt that American agriculture, proficient as it is, can be "drought resistant" in any major sense.

Regardless of their views on the existence of a 20-year cycle and the drought resistance of modern agriculture, many scientists are agreed on one important point: The United States has had a run of remarkably good weather during the last 15 years. And many think it foolhardy to expect that good fortune to continue indefinitely.

Dr. J. Murray Mitchell of the National Oceanic and Atmospheric Administration's Environmental Data Service is among the experts who believe that the world should be alert to the probability of change in weather patterns.

Dr. Mitchell, who is one of the nation's leading experts on climate change, says scientists have learned a great deal in the last five years about the fluctuations that have disturbed the earth's climate in the past. He also says there is no doubt that the earth is now at the peak of a very warm period. Change is to be expected.

The point made by many experts is this: World population has soared in the last few decades. World agriculture, adapting to the present norm, has only barely managed to stay ahead. The pressures of population and food need are so great now that the system has lost much of its flexibility. In such a situation, any change from the present "normal" weather could bring serious trouble.

"The normal period is normal only by definition," Dr. Bryson said in a recent article. "There appears to be nothing like it in the past 1,000 years."

Scientists Ask Why World Climate Is Changing

BY WALTER SULLIVAN | MAY 21, 1975

THE WORLD'S CLIMATE is changing. Of that scientists are firmly convinced. But in what direction and why are subjects of deepening debate.

There are specialists who say that a new ice age is on the way — the inevitable consequence of a natural cyclic process, or as a result of man-made pollution of the atmosphere. And there are those who say that such pollution may actually head off an ice age.

Sooner or later a major cooling of the climate is widely considered inevitable. Hints that it may already have begun are evident. The drop in mean temperatures since 1950 in the Northern Hemisphere has been sufficient, for example, to shorten Britain's growing season for crops by two weeks.

As noted in a recent report of the National Academy of Sciences, "The global patterns of food production and population that have evolved are implicitly dependent on the climate of the present century."

Vulnerability to climate change, it says, is "all the more serious when we recognize that our present climate is in fact highly abnormal, and that we may already be producing climatic changes, as a result of our own activities."

The first half of this century has apparently been the warmest period since the "hot spell" between 5,000 and 7,000 years ago immediately following the last ice age. That the climate, at least in the Northern Hemisphere, has been getting cooler since about 1950, is well established—if one ignores the last two winters.

It had been forecast by some specialists that last winter would be exceptionally cold, but as all ice skaters know, it was unusually mild in the New York area. In Boston it was the warmest in 22 years and in Moscow it was the second warmest in 230 years.

A major problem in seeking to assess the trend is to distinguish year-to-year fluctuations from those spread over decades, centuries and thousands of years.

Lack of agreement as to the factors that control climate change make it particularly difficult to assess current trends. Of major importance, therefore, is the debate as to the cause of such changes and the role of human activity in bringing them about, Among the major hypotheses are the following:

1. SOLAR ENERGY VARIATIONS

The amount of solar energy reaching the earth's surface at any one place and time of year varies because of changes in the earth's orbit and the tilt of its spin axis (The extent of that tilt determines the extent of seasonal changes).

There are also slight variations in the amount of energy radiated by the sun. They follow the 11-year sunspot cycle and relate chiefly to solar ultraviolet radiation.

Dr. Walter Orr Roberts, former head of the National Center for Atmospheric Research in Boulder, Colo., believes he has found a correlation between this cycle and weather phenomena such as jetstream behavior and droughts in the high plains east of the Rocky Mountains.

The droughts, he believes, tend to occur either in step with the 11-year cycle or with one of 20 to 22 years.

Such links are doubted by Dr. J. Murray Mitchell Jr., climatologist at the National Oceanic and Atmospheric Administration's Environmental Data Service. He sees no plausible explanation of how such slight variations in solar energy could affect the massive weather phenomena responsible for droughts and floods.

Tree-ring data from Nebraska and South Dakota, according to Dr. Mitchell, show that the pattern to which Dr. Roberts refers applies only to the last century, whereas earlier — as far back as the 16th century — major droughts occurred at irregular intervals generally longer than 20 years.

Triggering of the ice ages by cyclic changes of the earth's spin axis and orbit was proposed as early as the nineteen twenties by a Yugoslav, Milutin Milankovitch. Because of tugging by the gravity of other planets, the orbit of the earth changes shape. Sometimes it is virtually circular. At other periods the earth's distance from the sun varies during each year by several million miles.

At present, 6 per cent more solar radiation reaches the earth on Jan. 14 than it does six months earlier or later, tempering northern winters. This variation in the shape of the orbit occurs in a cycle of about 93,000 years.

The tilt of the spin axis with respect to the earth's orbit around the sun varies 22.0 to 24.5 degrees over a period of some 41,000 years. The aim of the axis with respect to the stars also rotates once every 26,000 years, causing precession of the equinoxes.

For many years the combined effects of these variations seemed too subtle to account for the ice ages, but recent discoveries have won converts for modernized versions of the Milankovitch thesis.

From the chemical composition of Pacific sediments, from studies of soil types in Central Europe and from fossil plankton that lived in the Caribbean it has been shown that in the last million years there have been considerably more ice ages than previously supposed.

According to the classic timetable, four great ice ages occurred. However, the new records of global climate show seven extraordinarily abrupt changes in the last million years. As noted in the academy report, they represent transition, in a few centuries, "from full glacial to full interglacial conditions."

Many scientists now consider it established that expansions of glaciers in the Southern Hemisphere coincided with the northern ice ages. Land areas, however, are meager in southern latitudes comparable to those that were heavily glaciated in the north.

Dr. George J. Kukla of Columbia University's Lamont-Doherty Geological Observatory lab proposed a way in which small variations in solar energy falling on the middle latitudes — as in the Milankovitch concept — could affect the climate.

It is the extent to which northern seas and land areas become covered with snow and ice in the fall. When such cover is extensive, as in the fall of 1971, the white surface reflects sunlight back into space and there is a reduction in heating of the atmosphere.

This prolongs the northern winter and cools the globe. In 1971, according to images from earth satellites, autumn snow and ice cover increased by 1.5 million square miles.

The following year was one of freak weather throughout much of the world: The winter was exceptionally cold in North America, the Mediterranean and other areas. Severe drought struck many parts of Asia and Europe.

The implication was that a change in solar input that was slight, but sufficient to increase autumn snow and ice cover substantially, could eventually lead to a major climate change.

From a reworking of the Milankovitch calculations Dr. Kukla has found that solar energy falling on the atmosphere in the autumn hit a minimum 17,000 years ago, at the height of the last ice age. It reached a maximum some 6,000 years ago, when the world became warmest since the last ice age.

While the theory is, as yet, far from being a full explanation for climate changes it suggests, he said, that a trend toward cooling will continue for the next 4,000 years even though, since 1973, autumn snow cover has diminished somewhat.

2. PENDULUM SWINGS

Some scientists believe that the ice ages are a product of cyclic phenomena affecting the flow of heat from the tropics to the polar regions through the sea and air.

Most of the solar energy that enters the oceans and drives the winds is received in the tropics and carried poleward. The polar regions radiate more energy into space than they receive from the sun, but ocean currents and winds bring in enough heat — or almost enough — to make up the deficit.

Until a few years ago some persons suspected that the presence or absence of pack ice covering the Arctic Ocean might play a key role in this delicately balanced process. An absence of pack ice, when ocean currents were carrying considerable heat into that ocean, would allow evaporation and the resulting moist winds would shed the snows of an ice age. Periodic freezing of the ocean would end the glaciation.

Recently, however, sediment samples extracted from the floor of the Arctic Ocean have shown that it was apparently never free of ice between the ice ages, even though before they began that ocean does appear to have been open.

In fact, according to Dr. F. Kenneth Hare, professor of geography at the University of Toronto, fossils from the Arctic islands of Canada, the Soviet Union and from Greenland all indicate an icefree ocean with "luxuriant" forests along its shores.

Another proposal regarding built-in pendulum swings of climate is that of Dr. Reginald E. Newell, professor of meteorology at the Massachusetts Institute of Technology. He believes ice ages are initiated when energy losses at high latitudes exceed energy gains in the tropics — a state that may exist at present.

An ice age ends, in this concept, when enough of the ocean becomes ice covered to curtail the escape of heat being carried poleward by ocean currents. At the present stage of such a cycle, he said in a recent article, surface water in polar seas would, be growing cooler, "in the slow process that will lead to the next ice age."

In a recent issue of the British journal Nature, Drs. Reid A. Bryson and E. W. Wahl of the Center for Climate Research at the University of Wisconsin cite records from nine North Atlantic weather ships indicating that from 1951 to the 1968 — 1972 period surface water temperatures dropped steadily.

The fall was comparable, they reported, to a return to the "Little Ice Age" that existed from 1430 to 1850. It was early in this period that pack ice apparently isolated the Norse colony in Greenland and led to its extinction. The temperature drop in the North Atlantic carried it one sixth of the way to the level of a fullfledged ice age, according to Drs. Bryson and Wahl.

Unfortunately, they said, several of these weather stations are being discontinued so that monitoring future trends will be difficult. Dr. Bryson attributes recent droughts in Africa and elsewhere to a southward displacement of the rain-bearing monsoons.

A similar change occurred in about 1600 B.C., he believes. The monsoon rains no longer reached northwest India. Fresh water lakes that had been there for 7,000 years dried into salt beds and the Indus Empire that had spread over the region for 1,500 years was destroyed.

3. MAN-MADE INFLUENCE

There is general agreement that introducing large amounts of smoke particles or carbon dioxide into the atmosphere can alter climate. The same would be true of generating industrial heat comparable to a substantial fraction of solar energy falling on the earth. The debate centers on the precise roles of these effects and the levels of pollution that would cause serious changes.

Carbon dioxide in the air acts like glass in a greenhouse. It permits solar energy to reach the earth as visible light, but it impedes the escape of that energy into space in the form of heat radiation (at infrared wave lengths).

Dr. Mitchell has pointed out that a variety of factors determine the role of carbon dioxide on earth. For example, the extent to which that gas, introduced into the atmosphere by smokestacks and exhaust pipes, is absorbed by the oceans depends on the temperature of surface waters.

This, in turn, is affected by climate, leading to so-called feedback effects. Plants consume carbon dioxide at rates that depend on temperature and the abundance of that gas in the air, complicating predictions of their role.

The observatory atop Mauna Loa, the great Hawaiian volcano, has recorded a steady rise in the annual mean level of carbon dioxide in the atmosphere, amounting to 4 per cent between 1958 and 1972.

That, however, was a period of global cooling — not the reverse, as one would expect from a greenhouse effect.

The Mauna Loa observatory has also recorded a steady rise in atmospheric turbidit — the extent to which particles overhead dim the brightness of the sun. The academy study finds that human activity over the last 120 years has contributed more to this atmospheric dust than have volcanic eruptions.

However, it says, the present atmospheric load of man made dust is perhaps only one fifth what was thrown into the stratosphere by the volcanic explosion of Krakatoa in 1883. The role of of atmospheric dust is complex, for it cuts off sunlight from the earth, but is itself heated by that light, warming levels of atmosphere in which it resides.

Until recently the idea that ice ages are initiated by intense volcanic activity was unpopular for lack of evidence for such activity. The hypothesis has gained more credence from the analysis of sediment cores extracted from the ocean floors by the drill ship Glomar Challenger.

According to University of Rhode Island scientists, ash was far more common in layers laid down in the last two million years than in the previous 18 million years.

If worldwide energy consumption continues to increase at its present rates, catastrophic climate changes have been projected by M. I. Budyko, a leading Soviet specialist. He says that the critical level will probably be reached within a century.

This, he has written, will lead to "a complete destruction of polar ice covers." Not only would sea levels rise but, with the Arctic Ocean free of ice, the entire weather system of the Northern Hemisphere would be altered.

However, Dr. Mitchell has suggested, warming of the climate due to pollution might be enough to head off an ice age "quite inadvertently."

CAN THE TRUTH BE LEARNED?

More precise knowledge of the past is certain to aid in choosing between various explanations for long-term climate changes. The

Greenland Ice Sheet Program, with American, Danish and Swiss participants, is drilling a series of holes into the crest of the Greenland ice in the hope, ultimately, of reconstructing a year-by-year record of climate for the last 100,000 years.

So far the ice has been penetrated 1,325 feet, extending the record back 1,420 years. The yearly layers can be counted, like tree rings, in terms of summer and winter variation in the relative abundance of two forms of oxygen (oxygen 16 and oxygen 18). Their ratio indicates temperature at the time when the snow fell to form that layer of the ice sheet.

The isotopes also reflect the long-term climate changes. A remarkable finding, reported in the May 1 issue of Nature, is that the trends in Greenland for the period 850 to 1700 A.D., closely match the British record for 1100 to 1950. California tree rings show a climate record similar to the one in Britain.

The implication is a lag of 250 years between climate variations in Greenland and those in regions east and west of the Atlantic.

If, in fact, the climatic cycles of Greenland precede those of Europe and North America by 250 years, a powerful means of prediction would be available. However, as noted in the Nature article, it is by no means certain that the effect is persistent.

The Academy of Sciences report notes that any assessment of climate trends is crippled by a lack of knowledge: "Not only are the basic scientific questions largely unanswered, but in many cases we do not yet know enough to pose the key questions."

The oceans clearly play an important — and little understood — role. Not only are they the chief source of water in the atmosphere but they harbor a vast reservoir of thermal energy. "When the dynamics of the ocean-atmosphere interaction are better known, according to the report, "we may find that the ocean plays a more important role than the atmosphere in climate changes."

The report, including a wide range of proposals for national and international programs of research, was prepared by the academy's

Committee for the Global Atmospheric Research Program, headed by Dr. Verner E. Suomi of the University of Wisconsin.

In his preface Dr. Suomi notes that, by the end of this decade, space vehicles will be able, on a global scale to observe the sun's output, energy reflected from the earth, distributions of clouds, snow and ice, as well as ocean temperatures. With these and other inputs a better understanding of how and why the climate is changing should become possible.

Scientists Warn of Expected Rise of Carbon Dioxide Content in Air

BY WALTER SULLIVAN | OCT. 13, 1976

WASHINGTON, OCT 12 — Over the next two centuries, increasing industrial activity is expected to raise the carbon dioxide content of the atmosphere at least fourfold and possibly eightfold, according to a report presented today to the International Council of Scientific Unions.

Because this could bring about major climate changes, it was termed "rather alarming" in the report, prepared by the council's Scientific Committee on Problems of the Environment.

The council, representing all the specialized scientific unions, is holding its general assembly at the National Academy of Sciences here.

The report, entitled "Environmental Issues 1976," notes that little has been done to implement the proposal for a global environmental monitoring system. The proposal was endorsed by the United Nations Conference on the Human Environment, held in Stockholm in 1972.

While analyzing the probable reasons for this failure, the report also examines possible long-term threats to the environment from human production of phosphorus, sulfur, mercury and nitrogen compounds. It recommends, as well, a wide range of programs to reveal which threats are real.

"It is difficult to see how best to improve the environment," the report says, "without first establishing fundamental facts: such facts will also serve to offset the interminable speculation passing for knowledge."

With regard to global monitoring it says: "Some of the proposed schemes are ambitious, idealistic, and very, comprehensive."

The hope was repeatedly expressed at the Stockholm conference that there be an international watch on the land, air and water of the earth to spot ominous changes.

The proposals included monitoring selected species of plants and animals sensitive to subtle changes in the environment, much as miners once carried canaries to warn them when odorless "fire damp" (chiefly methane gas) appeared.

The delay in implementation, says the report, may be linked to "deficiencies in our basic understanding of how to go about monitoring and hence how to build a comprehensive global monitoring system." A number of the report recommendations are designed to correct such deficiencies.

U. OF MOSCOW SOIL SCIENTIST

The 296-page report was prepared under Prof. Victor A. Kovda, who is a specialist in soil science at the University of Moscow, and his successor as president of SCOPE, Prof. Gilbert F. White, director of the Institute of Behavioral Science at the University of Colorado in Boulder.

Both men spoke at today's meeting, as did SCOPE members from five other countries. Dr. Kovda said he was "optimistic" but added that "we have to pressure governments, create social opinion," to get the monitoring stations and avoid an "environmental disaster:"

Monitoring needs are listed in the following categories:

• Measuring levels of potentially harmful or beneficial substances not only in air, land and water but in living organisms "including man and his food."

• Measuring such variables (or possible variables) as solar output, air transparency and soil chemistry.

• Recording the extent of beneficial and harmful effects on life of the factors listed in the first two categories as well as effects of such factors as crowding, disease and genetic variations.

• Keeping inventory of such indexes of climate change as icecap area, glacier size and sea level, as well as effects of deforestation, agriculture, urbanization and energy use.

The most effective monitoring has been that of the atmosphere, and this, the report says. has clearly shown the rise in carbon dioxide attributed to fuel burning, Carbon dioxide, it is feared, can act like the glass in a greenhouse, heating up the climate. Much, however, remains to be learned as to the extent to which oceans and the biosphere — the planet's living organisms — absorb the added carbon dioxide. The report calls research on this subject "a matter of urgency."

A special challenge, says the report, is to identify those threats to the environment that, once they become obvious, have reached an irreversible stage. An example cited is the fear that fluorocarbons, widely marketed as freons, will deplete the protective ozone of the stratosphere.

"Management actions" were initiated, it says, "based on models predicting the consequences of specific levels of emission, rather than waiting until such consequences were detected." Freons are used both as refrigerants and as propellants in spray cans. A ban on their use for the latter purpose now seems likely.

Worldwide Effort Is Proposed to Study Climate and Its Impact

BY THE NEW YORK TIMES | FEB. 13, 1979

GENEVA, FEB. 12 — Faced with little-understood threats to world climate that could catastrophically affect food production and energy use, specialists from around the world convened here today to consider the creation of a "World Climate Program" that over the next 20 years would narrow the uncertainties.

One goal of the plan would be to improve the understanding of factors affecting climate change and variability, using such projects as the one-year Global Weather Experiment now under way. That experiment involves observations with seven earth satellites, more than 40 ships and hundreds of data-collecting buoys, balloons and aircraft.

Another objective of the proposed project would be to extend greatly the collection of climate data, particularly in developing countries, and the application of such data to agriculture, land use planning, energy policy and water resources management.

The third purpose would be to study the impact of climate on society. In his keynote address at the opening session of the climate meeting today, Dr. Robert M. White, its chairman and a former head of the National Oceanic and Atmospheric Administration in the United States, said the project would try to determine why some social and economic structures are more resilient to climate events than others and whether these differences depend on factors "we can do something about."

The executive committee of the World Meteorological Organization, which is based in Geneva, has asked the conference to review the draft of an "International Plan of Action" for study of the impacts of climate on society.

Dr. White, a meteorologist, pointed out that while climatic conditions have fluctuated throughout history, mankind is more than ever at the mercy of such fluctuations. This vulnerability will reach an extreme level by the end of the century, he said.

"Conservative projections," Dr. White added, show a world population increase from 3.5 billion in 1970 to 6.5 billion by 2000. The United Nations Food and Agricultural Organization expects world food demand to rise about 44 percent by 1985 and 112 percent by 2000. Thus, Dr. White said, the world faces the "staggering challenge" of doubling its food production in 20 years. Success in this regard will depend heavily on coping with climate variability. Other speakers cited several examples from the recent past, such as the five-year drought ending in the early 1970's that brought famine and death to the region south of the Sahara. This was followed by a drought in 1972 that forced the Soviet Union to buy much of its wheat abroad, upsetting world grain markets.

In 1974, meager rains reduced food production in India. The following year, cold spells hit the Brazilian coffee crop with price increases felt by all American coffee drinkers. In 1976, Europe suffered severe droughts and the last two winters in the United States have been cold enough to force closings of factories and schools.

"These events," Dr. White said, "have demonstrated the sensitivity of international well-being and relations to climate events. They have demonstrated the fragility of world food production and trade and the extent to which income and employment continue to depend on the workings of the natural world."

Particularly ominous, he added, are the potentials for more radical changes, either from natural causes or from human activity.

Among the most serious concerns is the effect of increased carbon dioxide in the atmosphere, not only from heavy use of coal as fuel but from depletion of carbon reservoirs on the earth.

Because of forest clearing, there less vegetation to remove carbon dioxide from the air and the rate at which that gas accumulates therefore increases. Because of its optical properties, carbon dioxide acts like the glass of a greenhouse and could have catastrophic effects on climate.

Other major concerns include the role of substances released into the atmosphere that may deplete the stratospheric ozone protecting the earth from damaging ultra-violet rays. Such depletion could have uncertain climate effects. These substances include synthetics used for refrigeration and as spray-can propellants.

Accords have been reached in the United Nations to outlaw climate modification as an instrument of war, Dr. White pointed out, but there is no machinery to cope with nonbelligerent or inadvertent modifications. Hence, he said, there is an emerging need for "some mechanism to develop global environmental impact assessments that will be accepted by all nations."

Evgeny K. Federov, director of the Institute of Applied Geophysics in Moscow, said, however, that he considered it "scarcely possible" that the activities of a single country could alter global climate, even though it could affect regional weather.

Prepared reports are to be presented here during the first week of the meeting, followed by discussions to draft detailed findings and recommendations, including those relating to the proposed World Climate Program.

Increased Burning of Fuels Could Alter Climate

BY WALTER SULLIVAN | NOV. 20, 1979

WHAT WILL the climate of the future be like? Warmer? Colder? Few questions are more important to those who must plan future energy and agricultural policy.

Yet redoubled efforts to make even moderately reliable forecasts have brought home, as never before, the complexity of the factors affecting climate.

Those who propose that the world will grow warmer found recent support in an analysis of climate changes to be expected from heavy burning of fossil fuels — notably coal. The study was done for the White House by a panel of experts convened by the National Academy of Sciences.

It concluded that within a half-century such combustion could double the amount of carbon dioxide in the atmosphere and thereby warm it an average of about 6 degrees Fahrenheit — enough to cause major climate changes that conceivably could turn farmland to desert or make deserts fertile.

Carbon dioxide, like the glass of a greenhouse, allows visible sunlight to pass through, heating the earth, but absorbs infrared energy radiated from the earth as a consequence of the heating. It thus traps energy that normally would escape into space.

The latest report makes a persuasive case that because of this "greenhouse effect" the continuing rise in fuel burning, with the projected emphasis on coal and its liquid and gaseous derivatives, could have disastrous effects on agriculture. It implies that alternate sources such as solar power (if it can be made practical) and nuclear energy (if it can be made safe) may have to receive greater emphasis.

The doubling of atmospheric carbon dioxide by about 2030 is based on the assumption that the annual increase of 4 percent in fuel burning will continue. If the growth is cut to 2 percent, the report says, the doubling would be delayed 15 to 20 years.

The projected warming would presumably benefit some regions of the world and damage others. Any change, however, is likely to disrupt food production in many areas where agriculture is highly vulnerable to drought and other vagaries of climate.

One proposed effect of the warming, which would be most intense at high latitudes, is a spread of deserts from the Southwest into the Midwestern grain belt. Canada would become more hospitable to corn and wheat, but the soils left there by the ice ages are relatively poor.

Dr. W. Lawrence Gates, climatologist at Oregon State University in Corvallis, has proposed that a warming trend could melt the ice cover of the Arctic Ocean. This, he points out, would radically change weather patterns in north latitudes, resulting in an "environmental catastrophe." For example, precipitation patterns responsible for much of the world's food production might be altered.

Members of the panel that did the academy projection shied away from such speculation, pointing out that too little is known about the behavior of the atmosphere, its interactions with the oceans and other factors to make detailed projections.

Furthermore they avoided grappling with the possibility, raised by others, that natural trends might counter the predicted warming. It has been proposed, for example, that a warming caused by atmospheric carbon dioxide could be neutralized by a cooling due to long-range diminished solar activity. The sun radiates slightly more heat when it is most active.

Recently, Ernest M. Agee, professor of geosciences at Purdue University in West Lafayette, Ind., has suggested that a 90-year cycle in sunspot activity is entering a decline that has already cooled the climate over the past 40 years.

The view that sunspots are an index of energy radiated by the sun has gained considerable support in recent years. Such spots (associated with highly energetic eruptions) seem to have been almost totally absent on the sun in the late 17th and early 18th centuries. During this "Little Ice Age" there was great suffering in Europe and elsewhere when crops failed.

The report on carbon dioxide effects was prepared for the President's Office of Science and Technology Policy by a panel whose chairman was Jule G. Charney, weather specialist at the Massachusetts Institute of Technology. He has long been an investigator of the interaction of the earth and its atmosphere.

One key to assessing the problem, the report pointed out, is defining the carbon cycle — where the carbon comes from and where it goes. Atmospheric carbon has both natural and industrial origins.

It is currently coming out of smokestacks, home chimneys, automobile exhaust pipes and other sources at a prodigious rate. Since 1958, it is estimated that 78 billion tons of carbon from known fuel consumption have been discharged into the atmosphere.

STEADY INCREASE IS MEASURED

Precise measurements of atmospheric carbon dioxide show a steady annual increase since 1958, but it has amounted to only 42 billion tons, accounting for little more than half the amount discharged by combustion.

Where did the rest go? Some may have been incorporated into the vegetation of the world's forests, particularly if more atmospheric carbon dioxide makes them grow faster. In the photosynthetic process, plants use carbon dioxide and water to produce carbohydrates, the material of which they are made. But, says the report, despite speculation there is no reliable evidence on whether or not such accelerated growth really occurs.

The other (and presumably dominant) reservoir is the oceans, chiefly the top 300 feet, where mixing is relatively rapid. Below that is an intermediate zone, to a depth of about 3,000 feet, where vertical movements are slow and the carbon dioxide uptake may take decades.

In the vast, deeper reaches of the ocean the exchange with surface water is so slow that it becomes significant only over thousands of years.

A concern of the panel is that the role of the oceans as "the flywheel of climate" will lull policymakers into complacency. In addition to absorbing carbon dioxide the oceans retard any rapid change of climate because they are slow to change their own temperature.

In this way the heating effect due to carbon dioxide could be delayed until "an appreciable climate change is inevitable," according to the report.

Voicing a similar concern in his foreward to the report, Dr. Verner E. Suomi of the University of Wisconsin, chairman of the Academy's Climate Research Board which sponsored the study, says: "A wait-and-see policy may mean waiting until it is too late."

'FEEDBACK EFFECTS' ARE CRUCIAL

For a reliable prediction "feedback effects" must be taken into account. A major one, the panel believes, would come from water vapor in the atmosphere. If the climate becomes warmer, more water will evaporate, increasing the amount of such vapor in the air.

Water vapor plays the same heat-absorbing role as carbon dioxide. Therefore more water vapor will produce more heat and hence more water vapor. This is a so-called "positive feedback."

But again there are complicating factors: Increased low clouds could have a "negative feedback" effect in that they reflect sunlight back into space. If climate warming produces more clouds, they could then lessen the warming by such reflection.

A strong positive effect would be the reduction of snow and ice cover as the climate warmed. Such cover reflects sunlight back into space. As the climate warmed there would be less snow and ice, allowing greater absorption of solar energy and more warming.

An opposing view of the effects of carbon dioxide is offered by Bhaskar Choudhury of Computer Sciences Corporation in Silver Spring,

Md., and George Kukla of Columbia University's Lamont-Doherty Geological Observatory in Palisades, N.Y.

They point out, in a recent issue of the British journal Nature, that atmospheric carbon dioxide not only absorbs infrared radiation escaping from the earth but also robs it from incoming sunlight. Normally, such solar infrared causes snow to recrystallize in a way that makes it less reflective of sunlight. As a result, the snow absorbs more solar energy, helping it to melt.

But if carbon dioxide prevents this from happening, the snow lasts longer than usual, actually cooling the climate. The two scientists do not argue that this effect would necessarily lead to global cooling, instead of warming, but they do maintain that this factor should be taken into consideration.

"Obviously," they say, "we are far from a comprehensive determination" of the effect on snow and ice fields of doubling the carbon dioxide.

Nevertheless, they say that final assessment of the impact "is too complicated" to be judged, as it has been by the academy panel and others, by simple computer simulations of atmospheric behavior.

The academy assessment made use of computer simulations by the federally supported Geophysical Fluid Dynamics Laboratory in Princeton, N.J., and NASA's Institute for Space Studies in New York City. While the inputs contained various uncertainties and while they did did not lead to identical conclusions, all of them predicted a considerable warming.

A major area of uncertainty concerns the role of forest clearing for timber and new farmland. At present, according to the report, farms occupy about 10 percent of the world's land, while forests take up 30 percent.

In 1977 and 1978, several scientists here and abroad proposed that forest clearing was a major contributor to atmospheric carbon dioxide. Clearing leads to extensive decay that releases carbon dioxide; it also removes vegetation that would absorb that gas from the atmosphere. Some suggested the clearing might add as much as fuel burning.

This view has now been challenged by Wallace S. Broecker and his colleagues at the Lamont-Doherty Geological Observatory.

Dr. Broecker was one of those who, in 1975, first sounded the alarm regarding the potential role of increasing atmospheric levels of carbon dioxide. In the journal Science last month, he and his colleagues concluded that regrowth of previously cut forests and enhancement of forest growth resulting from the atmosphere's excess carbon dioxide has "roughly balanced the rate of forest destruction during the past few decades."

The Academy report says the actual effect "is poorly known." Estimates of the carbon added to the atmosphere by forest clearing since early in the last century, it reports, range from 40 billion to 200 billion tons.

CHAPTER 3

Scientists vs. Skeptics: The 1980s

Climate experts began to assert that action must be taken to avert the worst damage from global greenhouse warming. But industrial interests urged the American government to question whether climate change was really caused by human activity. Little progress was made toward curbing carbon emissions.

Warming of World's Climate Expected to Begin in the '80s

BY THE NEW YORK TIMES | JAN. 7, 1982

MANKIND'S ACTIVITIES in increasing the amount of carbon dioxide and other chemicals in the atmosphere can be expected to have a substantial warming effect on climate, with the first clear signs of the trend becoming evident within this decade, a scientist at the National Aeronautics and Space Administration said here today.

The changes are in prospect because of excess carbon dioxide put into the atmosphere as humans burn coal, gas, oil and wood and cut forests for agriculture and other purposes. More recently there has also been an atmospheric buildup of methane, nitrous oxide and other chemicals as a result of agriculture and industry, said Dr. James Hansen of the space agency's Goddard Institute for Space Studies in New York.

Dr. Hansen spoke at a session of the annual meeting of the American Association for the Advancement of Science here and amplified some of his remarks at a news conference.

Several recent studies have concluded that such a warming trend will occur, but the effects have usually been predicted for the next century and have been interpreted differently by specialists. Dr. Roger Revelle of the University of California at San Diego said the subject of future climate change produced by mankind's activity was shrouded by a fog of uncertainty.

Dr. Hansen said the probability was that a warmer climate would make some places wetter while others were likely to be drier than today, but that it was too early to say which effects any given region would experience. Several specialists have noted that a pronounced warming trend could raise sea levels sufficiently to inundate many of the world's major cities. There has already been a small rise in sea level simply because of expansion of the warmer surface waters of the ocean, Dr. Hansen said.

At the same session of the meeting, Hermann Flohn of University of Bonn said warming effects on the climate would be small at first, but, through the next century, might give the planet its warmest spell since an interglacial period 125,000 years ago. In that period, he noted, lions, elephants and other warm-climate animals roamed what is now England.

Scholars Ask for Action Now to Save Global Environment

BY PHILIP SHABECOFF | MAY 5, 1984

SCIENTISTS AND other scholars from around the world called today for concerted international action to protect the global environment and the biological systems that support human life.

At the end of a conference called the Global Possible and sponsored by the World Resource Institute, a nonprofit group devoted to seeking solutions to environmental and resource problems, the scholars called for international mobilization to deal with population, poverty, pollution, energy and "the erosion of the planet's renewable resource base — the forests, fisheries, agricultural lands, wildlife and biological diversity."

The conferees, who met on Wye Island on Maryland's Eastern Shore, concluded that "the future can be bright if the nations of the world start to act now to achieve a sustainable human society."

"If we remain inactive, whether through pessimism or complacency, we shall only make certain the darkness that many fear," they warned in a concluding statement.

The conference members declared: "'The era we are entering is new in human experience in that for the first time the human species has the capability to alter the environment on a global scale and within the span of a single generation. We are the the point where we must plan and manage our use of the environment."

GOALS FOR STABILIZATION

The statement established goals for stabilizing the global environment and suggested actions for reaching those goals. One key goal, it said, is easing the pressure of population growth and poverty through economic development. The conference also called for action in these other areas:

• Biological diversity. Noting a "historically unprecedented and accelerated extinction of species" — one paper said that every day another species becomes extinct — the conferees proposed that at least a 10th of the earth's land be reserved for parks preserves.

• Land resources. The statement said crop and livestock yield from good land had to be increased and losses of agriculture land to erosion and development had to be cut.

• Air, atmosphere and climate. "The dominant atmospheric problems are acid precipitation, ozone depletion and the risks of disruptive climate change from the buildup of carbon dioxide and other greenhouse gases and urban air pollution," the statement said.

• Fresh water. Although the conference agreed that there was no global shortage of fresh water, it said action was needed to make sure water supplies did not cause health problems.

NEED FOR BETTER ASSESSMENT

Other proposals included suggestions for better management of fisheries and forests, energy policies that remove subsidies for energy consumption and production and the development of renewable energy supplies.

The conference said one urgent need was improving global assessments of resources and life-support systems. "As we consider the contours of a brighter and sustainable future, its features become clearer," the statement said. "'World population is stabilized before it doubles again and the erosion of the planet's renewable resource base — the forests, fisheries, agricultural lands, wildlife and biological diversity — is halted. Societies pursue practices which stress reliance on the 'income' from these renewable resources, not a depletion of the planet's 'capital.'"

Man Said to Tax Earth's Systems

BY PHILIP SHABECOFF | FEB. 14, 1987

THE PRESSURES of population growth and economic expansion are starting to exceed the ability of the earth's natural systems to sustain such activity, a new report by the Worldwatch Institute warned today.

In its report, "State of the World 1987," the Washington-based research group said human use of the air, water, land, forests and other systems that support life on earth were pushing those systems over "thresholds" beyond which they cannot absorb such use without permanent change and damage.

The result has been declining food and fuel production in many parts of the world and, for the world as a whole, contamination of the atmosphere, climatic change, a mass extinction of plant and animal species and the long-term prospect of a decline in the quality of life, the report said.

"Many of these threshold crossings, which are making the earth less habitable for future generations, are taking society by surprise," said Lester R. Brown, president of the institute and director of the study.

THREE CRITICAL AREAS

"The most threatening globally are the depletion of the ozone layer, climate change and the loss of biological diversity," Mr. Brown said.

The report said that "so many natural systems becoming unstable within such a short period of time" could result in economic and political pressures that "could overwhelm the capacity of governments and individuals to adjust adequately."

The report cited Central America as an area where high population growth, deforestation, soil erosion and high energy costs have led to political instability and social disintegration.

It said "a frustrating paradox is emerging" from global efforts to achieve economic growth. "Efforts to improve living standards," the report asserted, "are themselves beginning to threaten the health of the global economy. The very notion of progress begs for redefinition in light of the intolerable consequences as a result of its pursuit."

"A sustainable society satisfies its needs without diminishing the prospects of the next generation," the report said, adding, "By many measures, contemporary society fails to meet this criterion."

DAMAGE FROM FOSSIL FUELS

The report noted that much of the world's economic growth over the last century has been based on the burning of fossil fuels such as coal and oil. But that activity, it asserted, was changing the atmosphere to the point where the global climate was expected to shift drastically in the next century, requiring vast adjustments in agriculture and other activities that will cost billions of dollars.

The report also said that although overall world agricultural production has been growing, it has been declining in many countries, particularly in Africa, because of soil erosion and the spread of deserts. Even in the United States, fully a sixth of the grain harvest comes from eroding lands or draws on diminishing sources of ground water for irrigation, and so cannot be sustained over the long run, according to the report.

The destruction of forests, in addition to accelerating the extinction of species, is having a heavy impact on underdeveloped countries such as India that depend on firewood for fuel, the report went on.

The report also addresses the future of nuclear energy in the wake of the explosion and fire last year at the Chernobyl power plant in the Soviet Union. The report concluded that the accident was pushing many countries to gradually phase out plans to rely heavily on nuclear power for future energy needs — a path some nations had embarked on even before the Chernobyl disaster.

It also said that the world was becoming divided along demographic lines, with the developed countries having stabilized population growth and most of the underdeveloped nations moving toward explosive expansion.

Mr. Brown said that the instability caused by many of these trends in areas such as Central America and Africa was of major political significance to the United States.

The report said the time has come for political leaders at the highest levels to address these problems. "The course corrections needed to restore a worldwide improvement in the human condition have no precedent," it said.

It added: "No generation has ever faced such a complex set of issues requiring immediate attention. Preceding generations have always been concerned about the future, but we are the first to be faced with decisions that will determine whether the earth our children inherit will be inhabitable."

Global Warming Has Begun, Expert Tells Senate

BY PHILIP SHABECOFF | JUNE 23, 1988

THE EARTH has been warmer in the first five months of this year than in any comparable period since measurements began 130 years ago, and the higher temperatures can now be attributed to a long-expected global warming trend linked to pollution, a space agency scientist reported today.

Until now, scientists have been cautious about attributing rising global temperatures of recent years to the predicted global warming caused by pollutants in the atmosphere, known as the "greenhouse effect." But today Dr. James E. Hansen of the National Aeronautics and Space Administration told a Congressional committee that it was 99 percent certain that the warming trend was not a natural variation but was caused by a buildup of carbon dioxide and other artificial gases in the atmosphere.

Dr. Hansen, a leading expert on climate change, said in an interview that there was no "magic number" that showed when the greenhouse effect was actually starting to cause changes in climate and weather. But he added, "It is time to stop waffling so much and say that the evidence is pretty strong that the greenhouse effect is here."

AN IMPACT LASTING CENTURIES

If Dr. Hansen and other scientists are correct, then humans, by burning of fossil fuels and other activities, have altered the global climate in a manner that will affect life on earth for centuries to come.

Dr. Hansen, director of NASA's Institute for Space Studies in Manhattan, testifed before the Senate Energy and Natural Resources Committee.

He and other scientists testifying before the Senate panel today said that projections of the climate change that is now apparently occurring mean that the Southeastern and Midwestern sections of

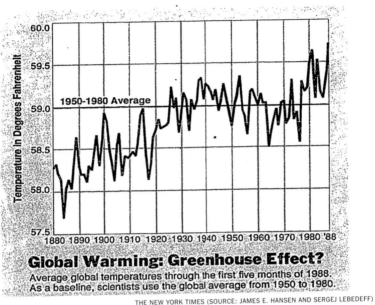

Global Warming: Greenhouse Effect?
Average global temperatures through the first five months of 1988.
As a baseline, scientists use the global average from 1950 to 1980.

THE NEW YORK TIMES (SOURCE: JAMES E. HANSEN AND SERGEJ LEBEDEFF)

Reproduction of a graph that appeared in the print version of this article.

the United States will be subject to frequent episodes of very high temperatures and drought in the next decade and beyond. But they cautioned that it was not possible to attribute a specific heat wave to the greenhouse effect, given the still limited state of knowledge on the subject.

SOME DISPUTE LINK

Some scientists still argue that warmer temperatures in recent years may be a result of natural fluctuations rather than human-induced changes.

Several Senators on the Committee joined witnesses in calling for action now on a broad national and international program to slow the pace of global warming.

Senator Timothy E. Wirth, the Colorado Democrat who presided at hearing today, said: "As I read it, the scientific evidence is compelling: the global climate is changing as the earth's atmosphere gets warmer. Now, the Congress must begin to consider how we are going to slow or halt that warming trend and how we are going to cope with the changes that may already be inevitable."

TRAPPING OF SOLAR RADIATION

Mathematical models have predicted for some years now that a buildup of carbon dioxide from the burning of fossil fuels such as coal and oil and other gases emitted by human activities into the atmosphere would cause the earth's surface to warm by trapping infrared radiation from the sun, turning the entire earth into a kind of greenhouse.

If the current pace of the buildup of these gases continues, the effect is likely to be a warming of 3 to 9 degrees Fahrenheit from the year 2025 to 2050, according to these projections. This rise in temperature is not expected to be uniform around the globe but to be greater in the higher latitudes, reaching as much as 20 degrees, and lower at the Equator.

The rise in global temperature is predicted to cause a thermal expansion of the oceans and to melt glaciers and polar ice, thus causing sea levels to rise by one to four feet by the middle of the next century. Scientists have already detected a slight rise in sea levels. At the same time, heat would cause inland waters to evaporate more rapidly, thus lowering the level of bodies of water such as the Great Lakes.

Dr. Hansen, who records temperatures from readings at monitoring stations around the world, had previously reported that four of the hottest years on record occurred in the 1980's. Compared with a 30-year base period from 1950 to 1980, when the global temperature averaged 59 degrees Fahrenheit, the temperature was one-third of a degree higher last year. In the entire century before 1880, global temperature had risen by half a degree, rising in the late 1800's and early 20th century, then roughly stabilizing for unknown reasons for several decades in the middle of the century.

WARMEST YEAR EXPECTED

In the first five months of this year, the temperature averaged about four-tenths of a degree above the base period, Dr. Hansen reported today. "The first five months of 1988 are so warm globally that we conclude that 1988 will be the warmest year on record unless there is a remarkable, improbable cooling in the remainder of the year," he told the Senate committee.

He also said that current climate patterns were consistent with the projections of the greenhouse effect in several respects in addition to the rise in temperature. For example, he said, the rise in temperature is greater in high latitudes than in low, is greater over continents than oceans, and there is cooling in the upper atmosphere as the lower atmosphere warms up.

"Global warming has reached a level such that we can ascribe with a high degree of confidence a cause and effect relationship between the greenhouse effect and observed warming," Dr. Hansen said at the hearing today, adding, "It is already happening now."

Dr. Syukuro Manabe of the Geophysical Fluid Dynamics Laboratory of the National Oceanic and Atmospheric Administration testified today that a number of factors, including an earlier snowmelt each year because of higher temperatures and a rain belt that moves farther north in the summer means that "it is likely that severe mid-continental summer dryness will occur more frequently with increasing atmsopheric temperature."

A TASTE OF THE FUTURE

While natural climate variability is the most likely chief cause of the current drought, Dr. Manabe said, the global warming trend is probably "aggravating the current dry condition." He added that the current drought was a foretaste of what the country would be facing in the years ahead.

Dr. George Woodwell, director of the Woods Hole Research Center in Woods Hole, Mass., said that while a slow warming trend would give human society time to respond, the rate of warming is uncertain. One factor that could speed up global warming is the widescale destruction of forests that are unable to adjust rapidly enough to rising temperatures. The dying forests would release the carbon dioxide they store in their organic matter, and thus greatly speed up the greenhouse effect.

SHARP CUT IN FUEL USE URGED

Dr. Woodwell, and other members of the panel, said that planning must begin now for a sharp reduction in the burning of coal, oil and other fossil fuels that release carbon dioxide. Because trees absorb and store carbon dioxide, he also proposed an end to the current rapid clearing of forests in many parts of the world and "a vigorous program of reforestation."

Some experts also believe that concern over global warming caused by the burning of fossil fuels warrants a renewed effort to develop safe nuclear power. Others stress the need for more efficient use of energy through conservation and other measures to curb fuel-burning.

Dr. Michael Oppenheimer, an atmospheric physicist with the Environmental Defense Fund, a national environmental group, said a number of steps can be taken immediately around the world, including the ratification and then strengthening of the treaty to reduce use of chlorofluorocarbons, which are widely used industrial chemicals that are said to contribute to the greenhouse effect. These chemicals have also been found to destroy ozone in the upper atmosphere that protects the earth's surface from harmful ultraviolet radiation from the sun.

Major 'Greenhouse' Impact Is Unavoidable, Experts Say

BY PHILIP SHABECOFF | JULY 18, 1988

MOMENTUM TOWARD a global warming caused by the greenhouse effect is now so great that there is no way to avoid a significant rise in temperature in the coming century, many scientists around the world now agree.

Even draconian measures to reduce the air pollution that is responsible for the global warming can only buy time to adjust to a warmer world and put a ceiling on the ultimate warming, these scientists say.

It is already time, they warn, to begin planning how to cope with the consequences of the increasing temperature and the associated changes in weather patterns, a rising sea level and other effects.

Yet strong measures to slow emissions from the burning of fossil fuels and reduce the ultimate temperature increase are also crucial, many experts believe. Without preventive action, they say, the pace of change will be so rapid that nature and human society will be seriously disrupted.

"What I fear most is rapid change," said Stephen H. Schneider, a climatologist for the National Center for Atmospheric Research in Boulder, Colo. The faster the changes, the more "surprises and imbalances," he said. "The effects on forests, and of sea level change, will be more damaging."

"But if the change is slow enough you can study the problems, determine what the regional impacts will be and learn how to adjust," Dr. Schneider said. "For example, you could develop seeds that will be able to take advantage of a longer but drier growing season."

Some Government officials and scientists are skeptical about the human ability and will to make the kinds of broad adjustments necessary to make a substantial reduction in the pace of global warming. Making the political case for painful countermeasures is hard because scientists still cannot say exactly what and where the disruptions would be.

And some serious conflicts of interest arise. How would curbs in energy use be divided, for example, among rich countries, which now burn the bulk of the world's fuels, and poor countries desperate to develop? Should countries seek to revive faltering nuclear power, which does not produce the carbon dioxide chiefly involved in the greenhouse effect, or should they subsidize conservation and solar energy? Will improvements in energy efficiency meet the need, or must ways of life be altered?

Given the costs of preventive action and the uncertainties about the benefits, some scientists and officials, including members of the Reagan Administration, argue that it makes sense to await more scientific knowledge before implementing expensive measures. There seems to be growing consensus, however, that the dangers of inaction outweigh the risks and costs of acting in face of scientific uncertainty.

One thing, at least, now appears clear to most atmospheric scientists. If the temperature increase is to be held to a minimum, there is no alternative to reducing emissions of carbon dioxide from the combustion of fossil fuels.

Carbon dioxide is chief among the gases emitted by human activity. The gases absorb infrared radiation from the sun that would otherwise be reflected back into the upper atmosphere, thus causing a gradual warming of the lower atmosphere and earth's surface. And among fossil fuels, coal, which is the most plentiful and the cheapest is the worst culprit. Gaining a given amount of heat from coal releases double the carbon dioxide than from natural gas, and a quarter more than from oil.

Other "greenhouse gases" include chlorofluorocarbons and halons — widely used industrial chemicals that many nations have agreed to reduce because they also damage the upper atmosphere's ozone layer — as well as methane from agriculture and waste dumps and nitrous oxides from motor vehicles, industry and fertilizers.

Some experts, including Dr. Irving M. Mintzer, a scientist for the World Resources Institute, a Washington research group, believe that the necessary adjustments can be made with relatively little pain if officials move quickly and aggressively.

Dr. Mintzer said the cuts in carbon dioxide emissions could be achieved by measures that would be desirable even without a global warming problem. They include cars that can would get at least 40 miles a gallon as against the United States average of 20 miles a gallon, more efficient light bulbs and electric appliances, urban planning that reduces traffic congestion, better insulated homes, and a halt to the rapid deforestation of the tropics. The clearing of tropical forests contributes to the problem because the giant old trees contain large amounts of carbon that are released when the trees rot or burn.

Other experts, including Lester B. Lave, an economist and environmental expert at Carnegie-Mellon University in Pittsburgh, do not think it will be so easy to slow the global trend.

"If anybody says they have an ice cream syrup recipe for doing it they are pulling our legs," he said.

'LESS OF A THROWAWAY SOCIETY'

Dr. Lave said that with a growing population and expanding economies, the world will need to consume more energy, even if it is used more efficiently. Realistically, he contended, that will require either burning more fossil fuel or a major expansion of nuclear energy.

Major changes in daily life would be necessary, he said. "We get to drive and fly less, and use a lot less fuel for space conditioning," he said. "Our houses can't be as warm in winter or as cool in summer. A lot of materials we use such as plastics and aluminum are really congealed energy. We are going to have to be less of a throwaway society."

Dr. Lave said that before people will be willing to make such sacrifices, scientists will need to convince them that they will suffer as a result of the global warming.

"If you really want me to give up my car or my air conditioner, you better prove to me first the earth would otherwise be uninhabitable," he said.

Perhaps the most difficult obstacle, in the view of many experts, would be reconciling global curbs in fossil fuels with efforts by poor countries to develop their industry and economies. Many of the countries, including China, the world's most populous, plan to base their economic growth on the expanding use of coal.

3 TO 9 DEGREES HIGHER

Delegates to a recent conference on world climate change, convened in Toronto by the Canadian Government, recently called for a 20 percent cut in global emissions of carbon dioxide by the year 2005, with the ultimate goal of reducing emissions by 50 percent. The world's population is now sending about 5.5 billion tons of carbon dioxide into the atmosphere each year, about half of which is absorbed by the oceans and forests. Thus a 50 percent cut in emissions would roughly stabilize the amount of the gas in the atmosphere.

But achieving such a cut in fuel burning in a world with even more people demanding ever better lives would be an awesome undertaking.

In the last century, as the industrial revolution exploded in Europe and North America largely through an exponential increase in the use of coal and oil, the concentration of carbon dioxide in the atmosphere rose to about 350 parts per million from about 274 parts per million. According to several mathmatical models prepared by scientists, when the amount of carbon dioxide reaches about 550 parts per million, about double that of the pre-industrial era, the average annual temperature will be 3 to 9 degrees Fahrenheit warmer than it would otherwise be. Such an increase would be outside the experience of human history.

At the current level of fossil fuel use, the doubling of carbon dioxide would be reached sometime around 2060 to 2070, according to several estimates. At the same time, other gases contributing to the greenhouse effect are also increasing, so the 3-to-9-degree warming may occur as early as 2030 by some estimates.

Such a rapid warming, by melting glaciers and causing thermal expansion of oceans, would raise the sea level by one to four feet. It would also cause disruptive shifts in weather patterns. So far, however, the global computer models cannot predict with confidence what those shifts will be.

BEST AND WORST CASES

Dr. Mintzer has prepared several different models for global warming based on different policies for using fossil fuels. If current trends in fuel use continue, he found, fossil fuel burning would be two and a half times its 1986 level by the year 2075, and average global temperatures would rise 5 to 15 degrees.

In the worst case model, in which the use of coal and other fossil fuels increases fivefold by 2075, global temperatures would rise 10 to 30 degrees.

Dr. Mintzer's best case model, which would entail substantially improved efficiency in the use of energy by industry, motor vehicles and houses, rapid introduction of solar and other renewable energy sources and a global commitment to restoring forests, shows temperatures rising 3 to 8 degrees by 2075.

Policies to reduce carbon dioxide would not be intended "to return to levels of a prehistoric environment but to influence climate change so it can be managed with minimum disruption of human society," Dr. Mintzer said.

Slowing down the rate of warming is crucial because it would give scientists time to find out what the problems will be and what responses are feasible and allow governments industry and individuals time to carry out those responses, Dr. Mintzer contended.

Dr. Chauncey Starr, president emeritus of the Electric Power Research Institute, an arm of the electric utility industry, said he doubted that the goals of reducing carbon dioxide emissions by 20 percent by the year 2005 and by 50 percent by the middle of the next century could be achieved.

'WORLD HAS NO CHOICE'

"Certainly everyone using fossil fuels should use them as efficiently as possible to reduce effluents into the atmosphere," he said, "but the reality is that most of the world has no choice but to use fossil fuels."

While the amitious goals set in Toronto may not be achievable, the rate of carbon dioxide emissions could be slowed by increasing use of energy sources that do not release carbon, such as solar, hydroelectric and nuclear power, Dr. Starr said. Changes in technology, like substituting electric cars for gasoline-powered vehicles in urban areas could also help, he said.

But Dr. Starr also suggested that some of the adjustments needed to reduce the pace and scope of global warming might not be worth the cost. Reducing the carbon dioxide emissions from electric power plants in the United States by 50 percent would buy "a year or two of time" in delaying the onset of the greenhouse effect, he said, adding, "What would you be willing to pay for that?"

But Dr. Schneider of the National Center for Atmospheric Research said the response to global warming should be based "not on economic judgments alone but on strategic considerations," similar to expenditures on national defense. Because of all the scientific unknowns, it is not feasible to apply cost-benefit analysis to the problem, he said. "But in my value system," he added, "prudence means slowing it down."

At the recent Toronto conference, Michael B. McElroy, chairman of Harvard University's Department of Earth and Planetary Sciences, said, "We face an immediate and important challenge: to understand and predict the consequences of our actions, and to bring this knowledge to bear on policy so as to preserve the viability of the planet for ourselves and for generations yet unborn."

"It is an awesome responsibility," he said.

Draft Report on Global Warming Foresees Environmental Havoc in U.S.

BY PHILIP SHABECOFF | OCT. 19, 1988

GLOBAL WARMING caused by industrial pollutants in the atmosphere is likely to shrink forests, destroy most coastal wetlands, reduce water quality and quantity in many areas and otherwise cause extensive environmental disruption in the United States over the next century, according to a draft report by the Environmental Protection Agency.

The report, prepared by the agency at the order of Congress, is "the first comprehensive look at the effects we might experience in this country from global warming," said Linda J. Fisher, the environmental agency's Assistant Administrator for Policy and Planning.

A second report ordered by Congress from the agency on policy recommendations for reducing the pollution that is producing global warming is due out by the end of the year. Scientists believe that the earth is warming because carbon dioxide and certain other industrial pollutants in the atmosphere tend to trap solar heat, a process called the greenhouse effect.

Although the report finds mostly negative consequences from global warming, in some areas, such as agriculture, the news is not all bad. The report concluded, for example, that while hotter, drier weather may reduce crop yields in some areas, including the Southeast and central portions of the country, it could increase productivity in more northerly agricultural regions.

RISE OF 3 TO 8 DEGREES

The 700-page report has not yet been officially released by the agency, but a 51-page executive summary was made available to The New York Times today by sources outside the Government. The report examines how the global warming trend is likely to affect the various regions of the country and their natural systems.

Scientists project that in the absence of major reductions in burning of fossil fuels, the major source of carbon dioxide pollution, the greenhouse effect will result in an average global warming of 3 to 8 degrees Fahrenheit by the middle of the next century.

The report concludes, "Global climate change will have significant implications for natural ecosystems; for when, where and how we farm; for the availability of water to drink and water to run our factories, for how we live in our cities; for the wetlands that spawn our fish; for the beaches we use for recreation, and for all levels of government and industry."

Agency officials cautioned that the projections in the report were based on computer models that contained many of uncertainties. They also noted that the report was still being reviewed for accuracy by scientists. But they said the evidence showed that global warming would bring major, irreversible changes in the country's natural systems.

MAJOR FINDINGS OF STUDY

Among the more significant findings of the report are these:

• Some ecological systems, particularly forests, which occupy one-third of the country's land area, may be unable to adapt quickly enough to a rapid increase in temperature. The warming trend could force the southern border of forests northward while the northern border moved more slowly. As a result the range of species such as sugar maples and hemlocks are likely to shrink. The composition of the forests is also likely to shift as temperatures rise and moisture content of the soil changes, making some regions less favorable to certain species of trees and more hospitable to others. The agency projects that the decline in the nation's forests will begin within 30 to 80 years.

• As the global sea levels rise by one to three feet or more because of thermal expansion of the oceans and the melting of glaciers, most of the nation's coastal marshes and swamps would be inundated by salt water. Louisiana, which has 40 percent of the nation's coastal wetlands, could lose up to 85 percent of these rich ecological habitats.

• Beaches and other developed coastlines could be protected by dredging and other means, but the cost would be high, as much as $111 billion through the year 2100. Even with these efforts, some 7,000 square miles of coastal drylands, an area the size of Massachusetts, could be lost.

• While changes in rainfall patterns cannot yet be predicted with accuracy, the warming trend is likely to produce changes in water quantity and quality in some areas. In California, for example, an earlier snowmelt and runoff could disrupt water management systems and mean that less water will be available in the drier months of late summer. Reduced snow and faster evaporation may reduce the level of the Great Lakes. Where there is less water there would be less dilution of pollutants. Higher temperatures could increase the growth of algae that would choke out other life in some lakes.

• Summer heat waves may lead to an increasing number of deaths, particularly among the elderly. This trend would be pronounced in northern states, where prolonged heat is now unusual. Diseases borne by insects, including malaria and Rocky Mountain spotted fever could spread as warmer weather expanded the range of the insects. Diseases exacerbated by air pollution, such as asthma and emphysema, are likely to be increasingly troublesome. Because hotter weather is likely to increase pollution.

"On a national scale, the supply of agricultural commodities does not appear to be be threatened by climate change," the report stated. The projections showed that while crop acreage in Appalachia, the Southeast and the southern Great Plains could decrease by 5 to 25 percent, acreage in the northern Great Plains, the northern Great Lakes states and the Pacific Northwest would increase by 5 to 17 percent. The growing amount of carbon dioxide in the air could actually increase the yield of some crops because carbon dioxide is absorbed by plants in photosynthesis.

RISE IN FOOD PRICES

Many of the nation's farmers might respond to climate changes by increasing irrigation or shifting to crops that thrive in drier soils. Food prices are likely to increase to the detriment of consumers but the benefit of food producers.

Some regions are likely to suffer more than others, the report noted. The Southeast, which would lose major lowland areas and already suffers from high temperatures in summer, is one region that would feel the effects of global warming heavily. California, which already has problems making do on its available water, would also have difficulty in adjusting to the climate changes.

Next month, governments of industrial and developing countries are scheduled to meet in Geneva under the sponsorship of the United Nations Environment Program and the World Meteorological Organization to set up panels to examine the predicted effects of global warming and to recommend strategies for dealing with the expected changes. The findings of the E.P.A. report are likely be considered at that meeting.

E.P.A. Proposes Rules to Curb Warming

BY PHILIP SHABECOFF | MARCH 13, 1989

THE ENVIRONMENTAL PROTECTION Agency is proposing bold actions for the next decade to delay and lessen the expected warming of the earth from industrial gases accumulating in the atmosphere.

In a report prepared for Congress, the agency is offering the first specific options from any government agency for mitigating the expected warming. Possible steps, the report said, were a sharp rise in car mileage, a similarly steep drop in energy use in homes, and fees on the use of oil, coal and natural gas.

The Bush Administration, Congress and the international community will study and debate the proposals before deciding whether to approve any of them. William K. Reilly, Administrator of the E.P.A., called the report "a very important first step to focus domestic and international attention on policy options for dealing with global warming."

MEASURES TO DISCOURAGE USE

The report, a copy of which was obtained by The New York Times, made these recommendations to deal with the so-called greenhouse effect:

• An international effort to require all new autos produced around the world to achieve an average of at least 40 miles per gallon of gasoline.

• Requiring all automobiles in industrial countries to install catalytic converters, like those required in the United States, to reduce gases from tailpipe emissions.

• Taking measures that would reduce the amount of fuel it takes to heat single family homes to half the amount used in 1980.

• Stopping net global deforestation by planting at least as many trees as are felled. Trees absorb carbon dioxide during photosynthesis.

- Imposing fees on coal, oil and natural gas to provide economic incentives to shift away from the use of fossil fuels.

- Accelerating research to develop solar power to compete with oil and natural gas.

- Sharply increased use of wood and other vegetation, grown on plantations dedicated to that purpose, as a replacement for fossil fuels in the production of energy. Vegetation used for fuel produces far less carbon dioxide than fossil fuels do.

- End all use of chlorofluorocarbons, industrial chemicals that contribute to global warming as well as to the depletion of the earth's protective ozone shield.

GASES TRAP RADIATION

The rate and magnitude of the expected global warming will depend on a number of factors. But scientists frequently cite a range of 3 to 9 degrees Fahrenheit as the most likely average increase in global temperature by the middle of the next century.

The major gases that play a part in the greenhouse effect are carbon dioxide — largely from the burning of fossil fuels — methane, chlorofluorcarbons and nitrous oxides. These gases trap infrared radiation from the sun that would otherwise escape back into space, and thus cause the surface of the earth to warm.

The report notes that many scientific uncertainties surround the timing and magnitude of the greenhouse effect. But a scientific consensus holds that the buildup of gases will cause substantial warming of the earth in the next century, and the E.P.A. warns that action must be taken now, not after all the uncertainties are resolved.

'DRACONIAN' MEASURES

Agency officials said that the recommended measures would not reverse but only slow the buildup of greehnouse gases. The agency did not propose measures that would stop the buildup because they would have to be "draconian," one agency official said.

One example of such a draconian measure, the official said, would be to bar all combustion of coal, which could have severe economic consequences.

"A lot more analysis will have to be done on the economic and social costs" of this and other options, Mr. Reilly said.

Senator Max Baucus, Democrat of Montana and chairman of the Senate Environmental Protection Subcommittee, said he would hold hearings on global climate change in early April, after the E.P.A. Science Advisory Board finishes its review of the report.

White House Admits Censoring Testimony

BY PHILIP SHABECOFF | **MAY 8, 1989**

THE WHITE HOUSE confirmed today that it had censored Congressional testimony on the effects of global warming by a top Government scientist, but it insisted that the changes reflected policy decisions, not scientific conclusions.

Marlin Fitzwater, the White House press secretary, said the Office of Management and Budget had changed conclusions about global warming data contained in the testimony of Dr. James T. Hansen, director of the space agency's Goddard Institute for Space Studies. He said the action was taken because the ideas presented were "not necessarily those of all scientists who have considered this matter."

In his original text, before it was changed, Dr. Hansen asserted that computer projections showed that global warming caused by pollution from human activity would cause upheavals in the earth's climate. He warned of substantial increases in temperature, drought in mid-latitudes, severe storms and other stresses.

But his testimony was changed to make his conclusions seem less certain.

In response to questions at the regular White House briefing this morning, Mr. Fitzwater said that an official of the Office of Management and Budget "five levels down from the top" had changed Dr. Hansen's testimony to reflect that "there are many points of view on the global warming issue and many of them conflict with those stated by Dr. Hansen."

But Dr. Hansen, appearing today before the Senate Subcommittee on Science, Technology and Space, said that the testimony he had submitted specifically stated that the conclusions represented his own scientific opinion, not Government policy or a scientific consensus.

He said he had been forced by the budget office to make changes that raised questions about the reliability of scientific evidence on expected climate changes. Another change imposed by the budget office made it seem as if there was some doubt that human activity was chiefly responsible for the pollution that, it is now widely agreed, will cause a global warming trend. This would occur as carbon dioxide and other manmade pollutants trap and retain heat from the sun in a process similar to what happens in a greenhouse.

"I don't think the science should be altered," he said in response to a question by Senator Albert Gore, the Tennessee Democrat who is chairman of the subcommmittee. "As a Government employee, I can and certainly do support Government policy. My only objection is changing the science."

SIMILAR COMPLAINT REPORTED

Another Government scientist testified at today's hearing that the budget office had tried to change his testimony on scientific issues earlier this year.

The scientist, Dr. Jerry D. Mahlman, director of the Geophysical Fluid Dynamics Laboratory of the National Oceanic and Atmospheric Administration, said that the changes proposed for his testimony on issues related to global warming were "objectionable and unscientific" and that the testimony would have been "embarrassing."

Dr. Mahlman said that he had refused to accept the changes in his testimony. "We in the scientific community demand the right to be wrong," he said. Dr. Mahlman said he prevailed in his effort to prevent the budget office from changing his testimony. Dr. Hansen said, however, that the budget office insisted on editing his testimony despite his strong objections.

GORE ASSAILS ADMINISTRATION

Senator Gore said Dr. Hansen's testimony was changed because the Bush Administration did not want to take action to cope with the expected global warming trend.

He said United States officials now meeting in Geneva with delegations from other countries were arguing that more study was needed before beginning work on an international treaty aimed at reducing the impact and mitigating the effects of climate change.

"President Bush, only months ago, told us he was an environmentalist," Mr. Gore said. "Yet, in the past few days alone, we've seen his Administration back away from a critical diplomatic initiative on global warming."

Mr. Fitzwater said President Bush's "personal view is that this is a serious problem that America needs to show and take leadership. But the science is something that still has to be sorted out. Obviously, the President hasn't made a judgment about scientific assessments."

The White House spokesman said that Dr. Hansen had a right to voice his opinion and that no punitive action would be taken against him for objecting to the changing of his testimony.

Mr. Gore said that if there was any retribution against Dr. Hansen, the Bush Administration would face "the equivalent of World War III" with Congress.

Governments Start Preparing for Global Warming Disasters

BY WILLIAM K. STEVENS | NOV. 13, 1989

IN THE QUICKENING international debate over global warming, the spotlight has played mostly on the question of how and whether to control the growing emissions of carbon dioxide and other gases that trap heat in the atmosphere.

Now another concern is starting to come to the fore as well. No matter what action is taken, some scientists say, there are already enough of these "greenhouse" gases in the atmosphere to cause a major warming, and more are certain to accumulate before the buildup can be halted.

As a result, climatologists, social scientists, planners and government officials are beginning to focus on how society might adapt to rising sea levels, shifting agricultural zones, changing climates and other problems that global warming would bring if it occurs on a significant scale.

Already, state and local governments along the coast of the United States are starting to plan for a possible long-term rise in the sea level, and a few have taken action to cope with it. In the Netherlands, planning is well advanced for an expansion of that country's system of dikes, dunes and other coastal defenses, and the Dutch are also offering their expertise to Indonesia and the Maldives.

Agricultural researchers are stepping up efforts to develop heat-resistant and drought-resistant crops that might gradually replace traditional crops if the climate changes.

And the electric power industry in America is planning how to meet the increase in the demand for power for air-conditioning that would surely result from global warming. In one of the first studies, the Electric Power Research Institute has calculated that for every 1.8 degrees Fahrenheit in climatic warming, power demand in the summer would rise 2 to 3 percent in the New York metropolitan area — enough to have a sizable effect on the region's limited generating capacity.

These stirrings are somewhat tentative, both because of uncertainty about the whole question of global warming and because of a tendency on the part of some environmentalists and politicians to play down the question of adaptation for fear it will divert attention from what they see as an overriding need to limit production of the greenhouse gases.

But reining them in is bound to be difficult. The world economy runs on fossil fuels, and burning these fuels generates increasing amounts of carbon dioxide, the most important greenhouse gas. Weaning the world away from them is likely to be a long and costly business. For developing countries especially, fossil fuels are tightly linked to prospects for development and a better life for their peoples, leaving those countries reluctant to give up the fuels.

As the difficulty of reducing greenhouse emissions has come home, the focus has shifted somewhat "from prevention to a focus on adaptation," said Michael H. Glantz of the National Center for Atmospheric Research in Boulder, Colo. Dr. Glantz, a social scientist, heads a group that studies the impact of climatic change on societies. And while a number of environmentalists, scientists and officials continue to believe that the first priority should be a reduction of emissions of greenhouse gases, some are now saying that adaptation must be considered as well.

In a report to President Bush earlier this year, the National Academy of Sciences argued that adaptive measures should be assigned a high priority. "We are already irrevocably committed to major global change in the years ahead," the report said, expressing the view prevalent among climatologists. "The elevated concentrations of greenhouse gases produced to date by human activities will persist for many centuries and will slowly change the climate of the earth, regardless of our actions."

Still, although many scientists agree on the broad outlines of global climate change, the system is so complex they cannot predict exactly how great the change will be or when and how it will affect specific regions.

This uncertainty means that in planning for a broad range of long-term activities like coastal development, construction of ports, location of waste-disposal sites, water projects and agricultural enterprises, flexibility is crucial, the academy told Mr. Bush.

In studying and planning for the expected impact of global warming, the Environmental Protection Agency is emphasizing this need for flexibility. "You've got to leave yourself leeway," said John Hoffman, the director of the agency's global change division.

The planning options for industrialized countries, with all their resources, are numerous, the academy's report said. But that is not the case for many developing countries. For instance, a one-meter rise in sea level, which some experts consider likely by the end of the next century, would cover broad areas of Bangladesh, Indonesia and Southeast Asia holding some of the world's largest populations and richest agricultural lands. Those countries, experts say, simply do not have the resources to deal with such a disaster.

Some experts, moreover, express concern that the industrialized countries, following a well-documented human tendency, will not take adaptive action until disaster is near, when it may be too late.

THE SCIENCE COMPLEXITY MAKES PREDICTION CHANCY

In the greenhouse effect, energy from the sun is trapped in the earth's atmosphere by carbon dioxide, methane, chlorofluorocarbons and other trace gases. The more gases, the more heat is trapped.

Carbon dioxide, the principal greenhouse gas, is emitted by the burning of fossil fuels. Scientists say atmospheric concentrations of all these gases combined have increased from about 280 parts per million of carbon dioxide at the start of the industrial age almost 200 years ago to the equivalent of 400 parts per million today. At the present rate of increase, scientists say that the level will grow to 570 parts per million, more than double the pre-industrial level, possibly as early as 2030.

Scientists calculating from mathematical models of the earth's atmosphere say this doubling could cause the atmosphere to warm by 3 to 8 degrees Fahrenheit. By comparison, the atmosphere has warmed by about 9 degrees since the end of the last ice age. But climatic and atmospheric change is so complex that there is great uncertainty about the predictive accuracy of the models.

How long it will take for maximum warming to be reached is uncertain because the oceans slow such warming. Most scientists expect the maximum warming to take place by the second half of the next century.

If change is slow enough, the Environmental Protection Agency said earlier this year in a report to Congress, adaptation may be manageable. But a sudden or rapid change, it said, might make it problematic.

SEA-LEVEL RISE DEFENDING COASTS IS A CONCERN

A rise in sea level is "one of the most certain impacts of climate change," the agency said in its report to Congress. Higher global temperatures would probably cause glaciers to melt, as well as leading to an expansion of the oceans because warm water occupies a larger volume of space than cold water. If levels of greenhouse gases in the atmosphere double, sea levels will rise; estimates of the average rise are from 1.5 feet to 6.5 feet. Some leading experts regard a rise of 1 meter, a little more than three feet, as most likely. They expect it to occur gradually in the next century, affecting coastal areas where about a billion people, a quarter of the world's population, now live.

In adapting to global warming, "the primary issue is coastal defense," said Michael Oppenheimer, a senior scientist with the Environmental Defense Fund. "Planning for sea-level rise must be done decades in advance of the actual unfolding of the consequences. If you're going to protect such areas with seawalls, or carry out a careful

retreat of populations, which will be inevitable in some cases, or protect houses, those are measures that must be planned many decades
ahead of time."

Gjerrit P. Hekstra, an ecologist in the environmental protection
branch of the government of the Netherlands, said defending a settled
coastline or coastal city from rising seas requires "a complete restruc-
turing of your hydrological infrastructure — ship channels, dikes,
canals, rivers, everything."

Dr. Hekstra's country has been doing that for many decades, and
the experience of the Netherlands may prove instructional for much of
the rest of the world. For the Dutch, adapting to a sea-level rise means
simply an expansion of the elaborate, modern coastal defense system it
has developed in the last 30 years. Government studies have shown that
to protect the country from a sea-level rise of 1 meter will require an
investment, over the long term, of up to $10 billion. The Netherlands has
already spent $15 billion on coastal defense in the last three decades.

Coastal defense means building dikes and piling up sand on the
coast to strengthen dunes and sculpting rivers and canals to keep sea
water from penetrating the soil and ruining both fresh water supplies
and agricultural land. Dr. Hekstra said it is his opinion as a private
ecologist that all this is well within existing technology and requires
only money.

"So I don't think your country and my country is the real problem,"
he said. That is not to minimize the problem, he said, since the United
States would have to spend billions of dollars to defend coastal cities
and developments against a one-meter rise in sea level and might well
have to abandon some low-lying regions altogether.

"We can cope," Dr. Hekstra said. "But not Indonesia, not Bangladesh, not Vietnam. They don't have the resources to do it. Who's going
to pay the bill for the developing countries?" In the United States, the
E.P.A. has made extensive studies of the effect of a rise in the sea level,
and most coastal states are beginning to plan for it. Questions being
examined include not only coastal defense but matters like beach ero-

sion and the intrusion of salt water into rivers and bays where it would foul drinking-water supplies. Possible solutions to salt-water intrusion include the construction of barrier dams in estuaries and canals to divert the salt water from drinking water intakes. Close attention is also being paid to the control of hazardous-waste disposal sites in areas likely to flood.

Most of the efforts are in early stages. But "I haven't talked to a single coastal state that isn't doing some hard thinking about this and where the government is starting to put together some plans," said Thomas W. Curtis, the director of the natural resources group of the National Governors' Association.

South Carolina, North Carolina, Maine and Florida, with sea-level rise in mind, have all enacted standards designed to control construction on their shorelines.

WATER RESOURCES SHORTAGES LIKELY FOR CALIFORNIA

Some predictions of climate change, admittedly chancy, forecast drier conditions for much of the American West, with serious consequences for a region where water scarcity is already a major factor of life and prosperity. The E.P.A. study for Congress, for instance, found that California's water demand could increase, even as water supplies decrease. The decrease would come about partly because more snow would melt in the winter and less in the summer. Since reservoirs do not have the capacity to store all the winter runoff, spring and summer water supplies would drop.

Experts say that a number of adaptive measures could help in such a situation. These could be as simple as lining irrigation systems so that less water is wasted or expensive solutions like building larger reservoirs or even such a harsh measure, should water become scarce enough, as imposing high prices on it.

"Despite a growing awareness of the problem, the institutions involved in managing our water resources are not really taking account of the greenhouse effect," said Peter H. Gleick, director of the global environment program of the Pacific Institute for Studies in Development, Environment and Security, a nonprofit research institute in Berkeley, Calif.

"The difficulty is that we don't know how precipitation patterns are going to change," said Dr. Oppenheimer of the Environmental Defense Fund. This, he said, underscores the limitations of adaptation.

AGRICULTURE CROP ADAPTATION SEEMS PROMISING

No more critical activity stands to be profoundly affected by global warming than agriculture, but scientists also consider it one of the most adaptable.

Almost all the crops now grown in the United States, for example, originally came from some other part of the world and were adapted to this continent.

Building on this tradition, the Federal Department of Agriculture is preparing to ease the way for whatever transplants might be required by global warming. Jim Duke, an economic botanist at the department's research center in Beltsville, Md., has been collecting data for some years on the temperature and rainfall conditions in which 1,000 agricultural plants flourish. He is now preparing to use this data in mathematical models of climate, which would tell what crops would adapt best if, for instance, New York's average temperature rose three degrees and its rainfall also increased.

The E.P.A. report to Congress said that warming might force abandonment of 10 to 50 percent of the Southeast's agricultural acreage.

"We might lose the conventional crops" in the Southeast, said Dr. Duke. "But assuming we didn't go dry, we would bring in semitropical crops. It's just a matter of selecting variety. We could bring in a wealth of tropical fruits and vegetables."

At the same time, agricultural researchers around the world have long been striving, through both genetic and cultivation techniques, to make many crops more adaptable to harsh environments. Gary Evans, a special assistant for global change issues at the Department of Agriculture, said, "We are augmenting most of our current plant-stress programs with an eye to what would take place if temperature or moisture shifted."

Researchers are also striking out in new directions with important implications for adaptation to global warming. At the University of Arizona, for instance, researchers led by Carl N. Hodges are experimenting with getting plants to grow in sea water. If they succeed, the technique could save fresh water in arid areas near oceans.

In Israel's Negev Desert, a team led by Yosef Misrahi of Ben Gurion University of the Negev is growing fruits and nuts at temperatures higher than 115 degrees. In the same area, the Jewish National Fund, the Israeli agency in charge of forestry and land conservation, is experimenting with a genetically improved species of loblolly pine, using seedlings donated by the Georgia-Pacific Corporation. Much of this sort of research is directly related to the prospect of global warming.

PROSPECTS SEEDS OF CHANGE IN HURRICANE

Even before Hurricane Hugo, Charleston, S.C., was attuned to two of the major effects scientists expect from global warming: a rising sea level and more frequent and more potent hurricanes. It had already required new buildings near the shore to be built far enough off the ground to escape flooding, which they did in the hurricane. The city had also begun installing pumping stations to insure proper drainage, unlike the situation with sewers that work by gravity, which do not drain when rising water covers their outlets.

But the hurricane certainly made a difference. "The hurricane deepened our resolve," Mayor Joseph P. Riley of Charleston said, "and made us more confident that our decisions along those lines were wise ones, and it certainly deepened our commitment to new ways of thinking and acting."

That, according to the conclusions of a study directed by Dr. Glantz of the National Center for Atmospheric Research, is how action to combat a long-term threat usually gets started. A number of case studies sponsored by the center found that a catalyst was usually necessary before governments would act. Once they did act, ad hoc responses were favored over longer-term, planned responses.

These responses, the study concluded, "have often built into the existing social structures an additional degree of rigidity" that make it more difficult to adapt flexibly.

Those charcteristics illustrate the difficulties of adaptation, Dr. Glantz said, especially in a situation so fraught with uncertainty as global warming, where the threat, however serious it ultimately proves to be, may not become readily apparent for years or even decades.

Skeptics Are Challenging Dire 'Greenhouse' Views

BY WILLIAM K. STEVENS | DEC. 12, 1989

AS GOVERNMENTS try to come to grips with what is widely depicted as a potentially catastrophic warming of the Earth's surface, dissenting scientists are challenging what they see as unnecessarily gloomy predictions.

The skeptics contend that forecasts of global warming are flawed and overstated and that the future might even hold no significant warming at all. Some say that if the warming is modest, as they believe likely, it could bring benefits like longer growing seasons in temperate zones, more rain in dry areas and an enrichment of crops and plant life.

In any case, they argue, it would be a mistake to take drastic and costly steps to limit emissions of carbon dioxide and other gases that trap the sun's heat in the earth's atmosphere until more is known about the problem. These "greenhouse" gases are building up as a result of human activity, especially the burning of fossil fuels.

MOST HAVE NO FIRM POSITION

Exactly how many scientists are involved in serious climatic research is unclear, but experts in the field say it includes fewer than 300 climatologists, meteorologists, geophysicists and people in related fields. Many of them, perhaps the majority, have not taken a firm position in the debate; they say that while the greenhouse theory is valid in general, there are too many uncertainties about its future effects.

Both of the other factions — those who believe global warming to be a clear and definite threat and those who say there is likely to be no significant warming — appear to be in a minority. Authorities on weather and climate can be found in all three groups.

Much of the dissenters' criticism is aimed at computerized mathematical models of the world's climate on which forecasts of global warming are largely based. The critics also cite data on past climatic trends, and they say the theory of greenhouse warming has not yet been fully explored.

"It's not that we have a bad theory," said Reid A. Bryson of the University of Wisconsin, a leading climate theorist. "It's that we have an incomplete theory with a lot of bad science being done."

FORECAST AND ITS BASIS

Most of the dissenters' assertions are being challenged in turn by scientists who adhere to the better-known view of global warming. This view holds that increasing concentrations of greenhouse gases are likely to cause the average temperature of the air at the Earth's surface to increase by three to eight degrees Fahrenheit some time in the next century, from the current global average level of 57 degrees. That amount of increase is generally accepted by a number of national and international scientific groups that have sought a consensus on the issue, including various panels of the National Academy of Sciences.

The forecast is based largely on what the forecasters see as the inherent scientific logic of the greenhouse theory and on the computerized simulations of the future atmosphere. The forecasters expect the warming to raise sea levels, through the expansion of warming water and the melting of ice around the world; to change the climate of the globe, and to disrupt weather, human society and balances among plants and animals.

Both the dissenters and those who call for action have been pressing their arguments in Washington as the Bush Administration grapples with pressures to reduce the burning of fossil fuels like coal and oil, which are the main source of human-produced atmospheric carbon dioxide.

Current forecasts of global warming "are so inaccurate and fraught with uncertainty as to be useless to policy-makers," Richard S. Lindzen of the Massachusetts of Institute of Technology and Jerome Namias of the Scripps Institution Oceanography in La Jolla, Calif., wrote in a letter to President Bush in late September. The two authorities on meteorology are both members of the National Academy of Sciences.

Their warning was one of several cautionary pleas now coming forth in the aftermath of months of speeches, writings and testimony to Congress by scientists and environmentalists who urge prompt countermeasures. Some important officials in the Administration, including John H. Sununu, the White House chief of staff, have also urged caution until further research is performed.

ARGUMENTS AND EVIDENCE: COMPUTER MODELS' ACCURACY DEBATED

Some of the dissenters, including Dr. Lindzen, say the scientific uncertainty could be reduced through a decade or less of intensive research, perhaps in three to five years. They counsel against drastic action to cut fossil-fuel emissions until then.

"The expense is patently obvious," said one of the most outspoken skeptics, Patrick Michaels, a professor of environmental sciences at the University of Virginia and a former president of the American Meteorological Society. "If the policy is going to be that expensive, the science should be much less murky than it is now," he said.

Other scientists have long acknowledged the uncertainties of global warming predictions, but argue that they will not be eliminated in time for effective action to be taken.

"My feeling is that the uncertainty will always remain," said Syukuro Manabe of the National Oceanic and Atmospheric Administration's Geophysical Fluid Dynamics Laboratory at Princeton University, a leading climatologist. Dr. Manabe's laboratory runs one of the major mathematical models of the global climate on which attempts to forecast future warming are mostly based. "We have to make decisions based on uncertain information," he said. "I don't think we have any other choice."

In view of the uncertainty, some scientists favor taking actions that would bring major benefits in their own right, like increasing energy efficiency and pressing the development of alternative power sources.

THE THEORY'S BACKERS

Among those who oppose dissenters like Dr. Bryson, Dr. Lindzen, Dr. Namias and Dr. Michaels are, for example, James E. Hansen of the Goddard Institute for Space Studies in New York City; Michael Oppenheimer, a senior scientist with the the Environmental Defense Fund; George M. Woodwell, director of the Woods Hole Research Center, and Stephen H. Schneider of the National Center for Atmospheric Research.

Dr. Hansen helped propel the issue of global warming to the forefront last year when, at the height of the 1988 heat wave and drought, he testified before Congress that global warming caused by increasing concentrations of greenhouse gases was already under way.

The climate models that draw much of the dissenters' criticism are mathematical equations that simulate the physical workings of the atmosphere. Scientists can insert any set of conditions they like — a given concentration of greenhouse gases, for instance — and a computer calculates how the climate would change, including changes in the average global temperature.

Global warming theorists maintain that a relatively small increase in the temperature can have major consequences. For example, they point out, the average temperature since the end of the last ice age has increased by nine degrees.

But the computer models "are seriously exaggerating the warming by at least two to threefold," said Hugh W. Ellsaesser, a meteorologist at Lawrence Livermore Laboratory in California who retired in 1986. He has been working on the question of global warming since 1972.

COMPLICATING FACTORS: CLOUDS
AND OCEANS POORLY UNDERSTOOD

All the models, said Dr. Lindzen, contain flaws that "could easily reduce the predictions for warming to well under a degree" centigrade, or 1.8

degrees Fahrenheit. Not least among the flaws, he and others say, is that the models fail to properly reflect the climatic effects of water vapor and clouds, which can each overwhelm the effect of the greenhouse gases.

Skeptics say that clouds might well reduce the warming by reflecting sunlight back into space, but some of the model experts say they could also, through a complex set of feedback mechanisms, increase the warming.

Clouds are poorly simulated in all the models, most climatologists agree. A team at the United Kingdom Meteorological Office in England reported in September that by representing clouds more realistically, its model had reduced the projection of expected warming from about nine degrees to about five. The British model has usually produced the highest estimates.

The findings have been cited by the skeptics as evidence that they are probably right in their contention that the warming has been overstated. But John F. B. Mitchell, the chief scientist on the British project, said the result did not mean that the group was cutting its forecast in half.

So little is known about the characteristics of clouds, he said, that even this latest simulation cannot be taken as realistic. Rather, he said, the result "essentially illustrates our uncertainty" and underscores a serious lack of data on how clouds behave. Without better data, he said, "we can go on doing numerical experiments till we're blue in the face and we won't reduce the uncertainties."

OCEANS' MODERATING EFFECTS

The models have only recently begun to reflect the enormous capacity of the oceans to absorb heat, a factor that scientists believe will slow down global warming substantially. Scientists studying a model at the National Center for Atmospheric Research in Boulder, Colo., recently completed a simulation that included the ocean's influence. It resulted in a warming of nearly three degrees when carbon dioxide in the atmosphere doubled, as against about seven degrees in an earlier model run.

This was also seen by some dissenters and Government officials as a one-half reduction in the models' warming estimates, but Warren Washington, one of the chiefs of the Boulder experiment, said that was a misinterpretation. The modeling exercise was not fully played out because of lack of computer access, and the simulation was carried only 30 years into the future, he said. If it had continued to the point where full effects were felt, he said, the warming would have been substantially larger.

MODELS AND MEASUREMENTS: BOTH SIDES CLAIM SUPPORT IN DATA

To some scientists who see themselves as neither dissenters nor backers of specific warming predictions, the uncertainties are perplexing and frustrating.

"Common physical sense tells us something is going to be happening" to the world's climate because of the greenhouse effect, said Robert D. Cess, a professor of atmospheric sciences at the State University of New York at Stony Brook, who heads an international group that assesses the models. But he said the group's conclusion, soon to be published, is that "we don't know what these models are doing." He said the models "as presently formulated" cannot be used to predict future global warming, and that "whether they can ever be used for that purpose is problematical."

Dr. Hansen defends the models, pointing out that even as they have become more sophisticated, their conclusions about global warming have generally remained within the range predicted in the 1970's. Some defenders of the models say they doubt that another decade of refinements would substantially alter the range.

Defenders also say the models have validated themselves by successfully simulating the waxing and waning of ice ages, present-day seasonal variations and the workings of the atmospheres of Venus and Mars.

But the critics say that the models have not done well at matching the climatic trends on the scale of a century. In the last century, according to some studies of temperature records, the average global temperature has risen by about one degree. Simulations by some models show that it should have risen by about twice that much.

To the dissenters, this gap casts doubt on the models' credibility. To some environmental scientists it shows the opposite. "We should be flabbergasted that the models can come that close, given the uncertainties," said Dr. Oppenheimer of the Environmental Defense Fund, a research and advocacy organization. The dispute on this point is muddied by the variations in temperature profiles for past decades that emerge from different studies. Some studies suggest little or no warming over the last century, depending on the data and methods used, and this has occasioned argument.

POSITIVE VIEWS: SOME SEE BENEFITS IN WARMER EARTH

Few scientists believe greenhouse warming can now be detected amid the normal swings of climate. But if it can, says Dr. Michaels, the evidence might be emerging from data collected by a team headed by Thomas Karl, a climate-change analyst at the Government's climatic data center at Asheville, N.C.

Studies there found that since the mid-1950's, nighttime temperatures in much of the United States have risen in fall, summer and winter, while daytime temperatures have dropped slightly. There is evidence of the same pattern in China and Australia, Mr. Karl said. He said the reasons are unclear, although increasing cloudiness appears to have contributed to it in this country.

"If nature is declaring her greenhouse with a relative rise in the nighttime rather than the daytime," said Dr. Michaels, "then the severity of the problem is drastically reduced." In fact, he said, warmer nights in temperate regions would lengthen growing seasons.

This could especially benefit northern regions, in the Northern Hemisphere, some scientists believe, and southern regions in the Southern. Some say, in fact, that countries like the Soviet Union and Canada might well benefit from even a high degree of warming.

RUSSIANS PREDICT BENEFITS

Two Soviet scientists, M. I. Budyko and Y. S. Sedunov, have said in a paper that increased rainfall over all the continents, along with the "fertilizer" effect on plants of carbon dioxide, "will considerably enhance" plant productivity, increase harvests, make large barren territories suitable for agriculture and permit the expansion of crops in other regions.

But Dr. Woodwell of the Woods Hole Institute argues that global warming would produce even more atmospheric carbon dioxide by speeding the decay of organic matter and accelerating the respiration of plants. This new source of carbon dioxide, he believes, would more than offset the amount absorbed by plants in photosynthesis. It could easily exceed the amount from fossil-fuel burning, he says, and cause the planet to warm up even more.

CHAPTER 4

Do We Have to Take Action? The 1990s

American coal and oil industries continued to fuel the skepticism about whether global warming was real. Europe and Japan began to take steps to reduce carbon emissions. Citing concerns about possible negative economic effects, the United States opposed taking such steps.

Bush's 'Whitewash Effect' on Warming

OPINION | BY JAMES H. SCHEUER | MARCH 2, 1990

IN HIS RECENT SPEECH to the Intergovernmental Panel on Climate Change, President Bush, who promised in his campaign to use the "White House effect" to counter the "greenhouse effect," delivered the "whitewash effect" instead.

Coming in the wake of the Hague conference, in which the U.S. was virtually alone in opposing proposals to cut emissions of gases that cause global warming, the speech was another example of his abdication of global leadership on the environment.

His top advisers reportedly were unanimous in urging him to take action to reduce emissions. They included William Reilly, the Administrator of the Environmental Protection Agency; James Watkins, Secretary of Energy; Secretary of State James Baker, and the science adviser, Dr. D. Allan Bromley.

Such unanimity is astonishing: for years, the Energy Department fought to protect the U.S. fossil fuel industry from E.P.A. forays. But this hard-won unanimity was overturned by the White House chief of staff, John Sununu, whose supposed qualification is a mechanical engineering degree.

Attacking "faceless bureaucrats" for trying to "create a policy in this country that cuts off our use of coal, oil and natural gas," Mr. Sununu defended his veto on the grounds of two beliefs: that scientific evidence was insufficient to warrant action and that antipollution measures would sap U.S. economic growth. The first proposition is dubious; the second, preposterous.

Days later, when eight prestigious environmental organizations sent Mr. Bush a letter criticizing his aide's action, Jay Hair, president of the National Wildlife Federation, said with exasperation, "The American people did not elect John Sununu."

No one denies that pollution has dramatically changed the world's atmosphere. What is in question, and fiendishly difficult to prove, are the effects of the changes.

Most scientists agree that increasing levels of carbon dioxide and other greenhouse gases will inevitably lead to global warming. But no one is certain how fast and how much temperatures will rise, and what the effects will be in any geographical area.

Scientific uncertainty does not mean we have to wait for more research to take action. We do not need to know everything in order to do anything. The relevant policy question is not whether the scientists are right but whether policy makers can afford to be wrong. Suppose we take reasonable, cost-effective steps to slow down global warming, and learn later the scientists were wrong and we didn't have to do anything after all.

Admittedly, we will have spent billions of dollars to reduce emissions of greenhouse gases. But, wisely spent, that investment will have brought us billions of dollars of benefits: reduced pollution, improved health, more energy-efficient cars, U.S. industry that is more internationally competitive and the creation of new global markets for American-made environmental technologies and services.

But suppose we gamble that global warming won't happen, and are wrong. When we have unambiguous evidence that warming is happening, it will be too late to slow it down.

Scenarios of sudden change — temperatures climbing three to five degrees in a decade — pose the greatest risks. Predicted plagues will come to pass: forests will die, crops will wither, oceans will rise, disease will increase. And we will be defenseless before them. Money in the bank, unspent to reach environmental goals, will then be cold comfort.

Mr. Bush and Mr. Sununu would have us believe we can protect ourselves from global warming only at the expense of economic growth. But Japan's impressive economic growth has hardly been stymied by its huge investment in some of the world's toughest air pollution controls and its development of an economic sector twice as energy-efficient as ours.

On the contrary, Japanese companies see environmental protection as a major market opportunity, and are aggressively developing and selling environmental technologies.

The "jobs vs. environment" argument is a myth handed down by an earlier generation of industrialists and long discredited. It deserves a decent burial, even by Mr. Sununu, who surely knows better — or should.

To Skeptics on Global Warming...

OPINION | BY AL GORE JR. | APRIL 21, 1990

WHEN ENVIRONMENTAL and financial experts from around the world gathered in Washington this week for a White House-sponsored conference on global warming, they expected a serious discussion. Instead, they were surprised and angered to hear President Bush wholeheartedly endorse delay and inaction.

Global climate change is real. It is the single most serious manifestation of a larger problem: the collision course between industrial civilization and the ecological system that supports life as we know it.

The purpose of Earth Day is to alert people around the world to that impending collision. And yet the Bush Administration, according to a leaked memo, is advising its policymakers that "a better approach is to raise the many uncertainties," and argue with other skeptics that nothing should be done until unresolved questions are definitively answered.

What are the skeptics' questions? Here are several of the most prominent. None of them stands up under scrutiny.

Q. *Aren't the dire predictions about global warming based on unreliable computer models? How do we know that there is any correlation between increased levels of carbon dioxide in the atmosphere and changes in temperature?*

A. The most compelling evidence comes from careful studies of tiny air bubbles in Antarctic ice. These show what has actually happened to the Earth's climate during the last 160,000 years. As illustrated by the accompanying graph, carbon dioxide and temperature have gone up and down in lockstep for as far back as scientists can measure.

Through the last two ice ages and the period of great warming in between, levels of carbon dioxide have fluctuated between 200 and 300 parts per million. Even the skeptics agree that concentrations of carbon dioxide will be pushed to levels of 600 parts per million within the next 35 to 45 years. It is irresponsible to assume that after moving in tandem with carbon dioxide for 160,000 years, temperatures will not be affected by those dramatic increases.

Q. *Do we know enough to act? Shouldn't we study the problem until we eliminate the uncertainties?*

A. That was the Administration's excuse last year, when it asked a distinguished United Nations-sponsored group of scientists to answer that question. A draft of the scientists' long-awaited report, leaked to the press this week, concludes that we must act now. The scientists say there's still a chance that the problem won't be as bad as they fear, but there's an equal chance that it will be much worse than predicted.

Q. *Come on, isn't this really a little far-fetched? After all, the Earth is a big place and probably has some kind of natural "thermostat" to maintain the present climate. Don't some scientists say that clouds or the oceans or sunspots will offset any effect caused by human activity?*

A. While the Earth is indeed vast in size, the atmosphere surrounding it is less than one one-thousandth the thickness of the Earth's diameter, a thin blue line around the crust of the Earth. Unprecedented population growth and new technologies for burning fuels, clearing forests and manufacturing chemicals have given humankind the ability to alter the composition of the atmosphere.

Everywhere on Earth, for example, each lungful of air now contains 600 percent more chlorine atoms than it did 40 years ago — or 3 billion years ago, for that matter. That chlorine is responsible for burning a hole in the stratospheric ozone layer. Similar increases in methane, nitrous oxide and other polluting gases add to the seriousness of global warming.

Q. *But how can we trust scientists on this issue when some of them say global climate change is real and some of them say it's not?*

A. Five hundred years ago, most scientists said the world was flat. Most people believed them because the Earth did indeed look flat. The new "model" of a round Earth was based on mathematical calculations that they could neither touch nor understand. Similarly, Galileo was punished for his then-novel view that the Earth orbited the sun, instead of the other way around.

In the last 20 years, eminent scientists continued to ridicule the theory of continental drift. The theory of global climate change used to be ridiculed, too. But in the last few years, the overwhelming majority of scientists who have examined the evidence have agreed that the problem is real.

Q. *Didn't NASA just report that new measurements of the Earth's temperature in the last 10 years showed no evidence of warming?*

A. That was the impression some people got. What NASA actually reported was that "nothing could be said" about a warming trend one way or another "due to the relatively short satellite data record." Temperatures naturally fluctuate so much from year to year that a single decade is not a long enough yardstick for a long-term trend. The decade as a whole, according to several other studies, was the hottest since temperatures have been recorded. The six hottest years on record occurred in the 1980's.

Q. *O.K., suppose temperatures do rise by a few degrees. So what?*

A. Even small changes in the average global temperature can have dramatic consequences. The last time there was a change as big as the one some now predict, temperatures dropped several degrees and what is now New York City was covered by ice one kilometer thick.

But this isn't about temperatures alone. It's about drastically changing climatic patterns that affect the distribution of rainfall, the intensity of storms and droughts and the directions of prevailing winds and ocean currents, which in turn dramatically affect our weather and climate. Some scientists say the first effects will be erratic weather patterns with extremes of heat and cold.

Q. *Isn't it easier to adapt to these changes than to prevent them?*

A. The changes could occur so swiftly that effective adaptation might become virtually impossible. The longer we wait, the more unpleasant our choices become.

We are in fact conducting a massive, unprecedented — some say unethical — experiment with consequences for all future generations. As you make your choice, bear in mind that you're choosing not only for your own generation but for your grandchildren as well. And remember too that our abuse of the environment could lead to the extinction of more than half of all species within the lifetimes of our children.

Q. *Isn't the cost of preventing this problem too high?*

A. Many of the solutions, such as eliminating subsidies for clear-cutting forests, actually save money. In any event, the costs of inaction are much higher, even if the skeptics refuse to measure them.

Q. *The changes you say are needed are too sweeping to be politically possible.*

A. What if I had asked you six months ago to assess the possibility that people in every country in Eastern Europe would abandon Communism, sing "We Shall Overcome" and embrace democracy within 90 days? Would you have called that "unlikely?" We all would have. But it happened because people changed their way of thinking about Communism.

People are changing their thinking about the importance of protecting the global environment. We too are showing our willingness to act. The obstacles may seem immovable, but so did the Berlin wall. With bold leadership and a new political "ecolibrium," we too shall overcome.

Loss of Tropical Forests Is Found Much Worse Than Was Thought

BY PHILIP SHABECOFF | JUNE 7, 1990

TROPICAL FORESTS, which play a vital role in regulating the global climate, are disappearing much more rapidly than previously estimated, an international research group said today.

Each year recently, 40 million to 50 million acres of tropical forest, an area the size of Washington State, has been vanishing as trees are cut for timber and to clear land for agriculture and other development, the World Resources Institute said in a report. The group said 1.9 billion acres of tropical forest remained.

The report, "World Resources 1990-91," prepared in collaboration with the United Nations, was described by its authors as the first comprehensive estimate in a decade of tropical-forest losses around the world.

The rate of loss, measured in most countries in 1987, was nearly 50 percent greater than the last global estimate, prepared by the United Nations Food and Agricultural Organization in 1980, according to the institute.

"We were startled to uncover this rate of global deforestation," said James Gustave Speth, president of the institute, a nonprofit Washington-based research and policy organization that specialized in environmental issues. "We were saying we were losing the forests at an acre a second, but it is much closer to an acre and a half a second."

The disappearance of tropical forests is regarded by environmental experts as one of the most serious global environmental problems. Through photosynthesis, the forests absorb huge quantities of carbon dioxide, the most important of the gases that are accumulating in the atmosphere. Many scientists believe that carbon dioxide, if not kept in check, will cause a significant warming of the earth in the next century, through a process known as the greenhouse effect.

FROM SATELLITE DATA

The report on forests was based on remote sensing data from National Oceanic and Atmospheric Administration and Landsat satellites that was orginally analyzed by each of the affected tropical countries. Dr. Allen L. Hammond, editor in chief of the report, said at a news conference here that for most of the countries the satellite data covered 1987, but for Brazil it covered 1988, since newer data were available for that country.

He said the estimates of actual forest loss were "very conservative," and that the actually losses probably were considerably higher.

The group's report said that in nine major tropical countries, the estimates of total annual losses of tropical-forest acreage were about four times as high as estimates from the years 1981 to 1985. The nine countries were Brazil, India, Indonesia, Vietnam, Thailand, the Philippines, Costa Rica, Cameroon and Myanmar (formerly Burma). Dr. Hammond said, however, that in Brazil, the rate of deforestation declined in 1988 from 1987, largely because the levels from the latter year were the highest on record.

As the tropical forests shrink, their capacity to absorb carbon dioxide declines, hastening the onset and increasing the magnitude of the warming phenomenon. And as the vegetation from the cut forests decays or is burned, it emits more carbon dioxide.

The tropical forests also contain the largest and most diverse populations of plant and animal species of any habitat. As the forests vanish, so do many of these species, many before they ever have been discovered, named and analyzed.

Tropical forests have infertile soil because most of the nutrients are in the vegetation, not the soil. Thus, when these forests are cleared they tend to regenerate slowly, if at all.

'AN UNPARALLELED TRAGEDY'

"Tropical deforestation is an unparalleled tragedy," said Mr. Speth. "If we don't reverse the trend soon, it will be too late."

Senator Patrick Leahy, Democrat of Vermont and chairman of the Senate Agriculture Committee, said in a statement: "This is the first reliable data we've had on tropical deforestation in 10 years. A situation we knew was bleak is now shown to be truly horrendous."

The World Resources Institute report was prepared in collaboration with the United Nations Environment Program and the United Nations Development Program. Joan Martin Brown, special adviser to the executive director of the United Nations Environment Program, said at the news conference that her organization did not have its own capacity to do the kind of research contained in the report.

Since preagricultural times, the report said, the world has lost about one-fifth of all its forests, from more than 12 billion acres to under 10 billion acres. In the past, most of the losses were in the temperate forests of Europe, Asia and North America. In recent years, however, it is the tropical forests of the developing countries of Latin America, Asia and Africa that have been disappearing most rapidly.

FORESTS WITHOUT TREES

Brazil, with the largest remaining tropical forest area, is also experiencing the worst losses — between 12.5 million and 22.5 million acres a year, the report found. Myanamar is losing 1.7 million acres a year, more than 500 times the 1980 estimate by the Food and Agricultural Organization.

India, according to the data, is losing its forests at a rate of 3.7 million acres a year. Large areas legally designated as forest land "are already virtually treeless," the report said. Indonesia is losing 2.2 million acres a year, and Costa Rica 300,000 acres, both substantially more than the 1980 estimate.

The problem of deforestation in developing countries "has been exacerbated by government economic, land tenure and agricultural policies as well as population pressures, poverty and debt," the report said.

The World Resources report also contains a new index of countries that are the greatest net contributors to the atmosphere of carbon dioxide, chlorofluorcarbons and methane, the major gases contributing to global warming.

SURPRISES ON LIST

The United States and the Soviet Union are the first and second-largest net producers of these greenhouse gases, the report found. It added that if the European Community were considered a single country, it would rank second behind the United States.

But the next three countries on the index, surprisingly, were developing nations, Brazil, China and India.

It has been widely believed that the industrialized countries are the main producers of greenhouse gases. But the research group found that the developing countries already account for 45 percent of emissions of these gases, and that their contribution is likely to rise sharply as they consume more energy for industrial development.

While there is still uncertainty about global warming, Mr. Speth said, the scientific consensus is that "the risks of global climate change are very real and it would be very shortsighted to conclude otherwise."

"The conclusion of the great bulk of credible scientists is that enough is known to act now," said Mr. Speth, who was chairman of the Council on Environmental Quality in the Carter Administration. "It is our view that it is already late."

Thinning Arctic Ice

THE NEW YORK TIMES | **JULY 9, 1990**

SURVEYS BY SUBMARINES have turned up evidence that ice in the Arctic Ocean may have been thinner in the 1980's than in the 1970's, and scientists have tentatively raised the possibility that the thinning might have been caused by global warming.

Peter Wadhams, a scientist at the Scott Polar Research Institute at Cambridge University in England, compared the results of ice studies carried out by sonar aboard British submarines in 1976 and 1987. He reported in a recent issue of Nature that in a zone extending about 250 miles north of Greenland, the ice was significantly thinner at the end of the period. The thinning resulted in a loss of more than 15 percent of the ice over an area of more than 185,000 square miles.

Among the factors that could have caused the thinning, Dr. Wadhams wrote, is global warming produced by the greenhouse effect, in which increasing amounts of carbon dioxide, much of it from the burning of fossil fuels, traps more heat in the atmosphere. But he also cited other possible causes, mainly changes caused by shifts in wind patterns.

The findings were called provocative in an accompanying commentary, whose chief author was A. S. McLaren, a researcher at the Unversity of Colorado who specializes in global climate change and sea ice. But Dr. McLaren said in an interview that the tracks of the two British submarines did not coincide, that their cruises took place in different seasons and that the study did not take account of variations in weather patterns between 1976 and 1987. He and Dr. Wadhams agreed that more data were needed.

Earlier Harm Seen in Global Warming

BY WILLIAM K. STEVENS | OCT. 16, 1990

AFTER TWO YEARS of study, an international group of scientists working under United Nations auspices has found that global warming could cause serious environmental damage starting in the early years of the next century, long before the maximum temperature levels predicted by many scientists are reached.

And for the first time, they recommended establishing limits beyond which the average global temperature and sea level should not be permitted to rise, lest the world be subjected to serious and ever-increasing risks.

These limits are well below the levels that another international scientific panel said last June will ultimately result if heat-trapping gases, mainly carbon dioxide, continue to pour into the atmosphere at the present rate.

A report issued yesterday also includes a detailed analysis of measures that might bring the expected warming under control and concludes that if the measures are aggressively pursued, the limits can be achieved.

STEPS TOWARD FORMAL TREATY

The conclusions, recommendations and supporting analyses will furnish grist for the Second World Climate Conference starting in Geneva on Oct. 29, a gathering sponsored by the United Nations at which governments from around the world expect to take the first steps toward what they hope will be a formal treaty aimed at controlling global warming.

Two international groups of scientists have been studying the problem, both with United Nations sponsorship. One, operating as part of the Intergovernmental Panel on Climate Change, was formed in late

1988 to advise the governments attending the World Climate Confer-ence. The other, which was formed in 1986 and was the progenitor of the intergovernmental panel, has no government affiliation but rather is an association of independent scientists called the

ADVISORY GROUP ON GREENHOUSE GASES.

The independent group's report, issued yesterday in London, Stock-holm and New York, goes beyond the scientific assessment of the intergovernmental panel, made public last June, in attempting to set targets for the control of global warming.

Among the practical measures that the scientists said might be taken to limit the warming were improved energy efficiency, greater reliance on natural gas, reforestation and the adoption of alternative energy sources that are both technologically and economically feasi-ble. The sources include solar, wind, geothermal and biomass technol-ogies. "Limiting emissions so we can stay below the minimums should be attainable," said Michael Oppenheimer, senior scientist for the Environmental Defense Fund, who was the chairman of the working group on control measures.

RATE OF INCREASE FORECAST

In June, the scientists advising the intergovernmental group predicted that under what it called the "business as usual" scenario, the average global temperature would rise by nearly two degrees Fahrenheit by the year 2025 and by more than five degrees by the end of the next century. The rate of increase, which scientists say is as important as the absolute increase because of the difficulty of adjusting to rapid cli-matic change, was predicted at about half a degree per decade.

In the report issued yesterday, the independent scientists said that to minimize the risk of environmental damage, the rate of increase should be held below one-fifth of a degree per decade.

An absolute increase beyond 1990 of more than about two degrees above pre-industrial levels, it said, "may elicit rapid, unpredictable and non-linear responses that could lead to extensive ecosystem damage." Non-linear responses refer, for example, to sudden jumps in global temperature rather than even, gradual increases.

The report last June of the intergovernmental scientific panel said that the world has already warmed by about half a degree to one degree since the industrial age began, but scientists do not know whether this rise was caused by greenhouse gases emitted as a result of human activity or whether it is attributable to natural climatic variability and therefore, possibly, is temporary.

'SEVERE IMPACTS' WITHOUT ACTION

The report said that the atmosphere may already contain enough heat-trapping gases to push the global temperature above the two-degree target. "This means that unless we take very prompt and significant actions to reduce greenhouse emissions, we're very likely to experience severe impacts," said Peter Gleick, a co-chairman of the working group dealing with targets. He directs the global environmental programs of the Pacific Institute in Berkeley, Calif., a non-profit research institute.

The report established an "upper limit" of about 3.5 degrees in temperature increase since the start of the industrial age "beyond which the risks of grave damage to ecosystems, and of non-linear responses, are expected to increase rapidly."

While the voluminous study was reviewed in detail by other scientists before it was issued, not all authorities were initially prepared to give it unqualified endorsement.

"It sounds as if they've taken the worst-case scenarios and tried to make the case for a maximum effort," said William D. Nordhaus, a Yale University economist who cautioned that he had not yet had a chance to read the report. He has been the chairman or co-chairman of a number of National Academy of Sciences panels looking into global warming.

Scientists Urging Gas Emission Cuts

BY MARLISE SIMONS | NOV. 4, 1990

GENEVA — A group of scientists considered experts on world climate called Saturday on all nations to take immediate steps to control global warming, regardless of the many questions that still exist about man-made climate change.

The scientists, at the Second World Climate Conference here, completed their report late Saturday and made it public today. They said in a statement that the technology already exists to make substantial cuts in the emission of harmful gases without jeopardizing economic growth. The cuts and changes they are pressing for are far more drastic than any government is now considering.

But the unexpectedly strong statement, a consensus reached by more than 700 scientists and environmental specialists, appears to emphasize differences with the Bush Administration, which has problems with the view that governments should lose no time and set immediate targets for cutting back carbon dioxide.

THE U.S. POSITION

The statement is also expected to leave the United States further isolated diplomatically this week when more than 100 environmental ministers will conclude the conference.

In recent days, most wealthy nations, including the 12 countries of the European Community, have set targets for slowing carbon dioxide coming from cars, homes and factories, and some countries have even pledged to cut back on today's emissions.

The Bush Administration holds that it is still too early to decide how the United States, which is responsible for 24 percent of the world's carbon dioxide emissions, should reduce them, suggesting that to do so risks enormous costs and unduly curtailing its economic growth.

While the United States is not the only country that feels uneasy about assessing how man is tampering with the enormously complex system that makes up the world climate, it is almost the only industrialized nation that opposes committing itself to cutbacks in the present.

This week large oil producers, including the Soviet Union, Saudi Arabia and Venezuela, have rallied to the American side. Experts said these nations believe they will lose if the world suddenly starts burning less oil, the main source of carbon dioxide.

'BETWEEN SCIENCE AND POLICY'

Scientists involved in drafting the strong 13-page conference statement said the document would serve as the framework for future discussions and would be hard for policymakers to ignore. It carries the stamp of the World Meteorological Organization and the world's Oceanographic Commission and a number of United Nations bodies who sponsored the conference. It was unusual because it was the first official call for political action coming from such a large group of climate scientists, among them a number of Americans.

"We are at an interesting edge between science and policy now," said Maurice la Riviere, a professor of environmental biology and the head of the International Council of Scientific Unions. "We hope governments and policymakers will understand what scientists mean. Where we go from here is up to them, but given what we know, there is absolutely no excuse for governments not to save on energy."

The digression from science to politics in the six-day technical conference also made some scientists and specialists uneasy.

"There is a leap here from science to policy that is not comfortable for some people," said Michael Glantz, a social scientists at the National Center for Atmospheric Research in Boulder, Colo.

CHANGE AT AN UNSEEN PACE

Harmuth Grassl, a German professor of meteorology, said that while "as scientists we are basically here as ruminants, it is very important to get out the main message: That change on earth is now so fast there is no analogy during the last 10,000 years."

For its scientific substance, the conference statement drew heavily on the report released last May by the Intergovernmental Panel on Climate Change, which is now considered the most important assessment so far of knowledge available on climate change.

The new report issued here today included these points:

• Notwithstanding scientific and economic uncertainties, all countries should take immediate steps to reduce greenhouse gases and find more ways to absorb excess gases already in the atmosphere.

• Without such actions, global warming will increase between 2 and 5 degrees centigrade over the next century, a rate of change unprecedented in the last 10,000 years.

• This warming could lead to a sea level rise between 35 and 65 centimeters in the next century. Although the range is large, it is prudent to take precautions.

• It is now technically feasible and cost-effective to reduce carbon dioxide emissions in all countries. There are enough opportunities for many industrialized countries to cut carbon dioxide by at least 20 percent by the year 2005 if they use energy more efficiently, employ alternative fuels and plant more forests to absorb carbon.

Scientists also said to understand climate it was vital to expand global observation systems and above all establish a network to study the world's oceans. Scientists say the workings of the ocean, the main regulator of the world climate, are poorly understood.

Separate Studies Rank '90 As World's Warmest Year

BY WILLIAM K. STEVENS | JAN. 9, 1991

THE EARTH WAS warmer in 1990 than in any other year since people began measuring the planet's surface temperature, separate groups of climatologists in the United States and Britain said yesterday.

A third group, in the United States, reported record temperatures from one to six miles above the earth's surface. These were recorded from balloons from December 1989 through November 1990.

Some scientists said the new reports, taken together with the series of very warm years in the 1980's, strengthened the possibility that a feared global warming caused by an increase of heat-trapping atmospheric gases, had already begun.

These gases, chiefly carbon dioxide, chlorofluorocarbons and methane, are increasing, mostly as a result of human activity. This type of greenhouse warming could cause sharp changes in climate, agriculture and even sea levels.

Other scientists noted the difficulty of detecting the tiny initial signal of greenhouse warming amid the much greater temperature swings caused by nature.

"I would agree that it is of concern that we've had these hot periods," said Tim Barnett, a climatologist at the Scripps Institution of Oceanography in La Jolla, Calif. "But at this point you can't attribute it to any single cause. Is it the greenhouse gases, or is it natural variability?" He said it was impossible to draw any conclusion based on the average global temperatures alone.

The seven warmest years since 1880 all occurred in the last 11 years, according to climatologists at the space agency's Goddard Institute for Space Studies in New York. And six of the seven warmest years since 1850 have all occurred since 1980, according to a somewhat different set of surface measurements by scientists at the University of East Anglia in England and at the British Meteorological Office. The Goddard team analyzed temperatures recorded on land and on oceanic islands; the British team also included temperatures taken by ships at sea.

"The case for a cause-and-effect relationship" between the recent warming and a human-induced greenhouse effect "is becoming harder to deny," said James E. Hansen of the Goddard Institute. Dr. Hansen made a well-publicized statement in 1988 that the greenhouse effect was probably the cause of the observed rise in global temperatures.

A SKEPTIC BEGINS TO WAVER

His group reported yesterday that 1990, with an average global temperature of 59.8 degrees, was the warmest year globally since the records used by the group began in 1880.

"I wouldn't disagree with that," James K. Angell of the National Oceanic and Atmospheric Administration's Air Resources Laboratory in Silver Spring, Md., said of Dr. Hansen's comment. Dr. Angell reported the balloon measurements. "I've been a skeptic, but as these warmish years come one upon the other, you begin to waver a little bit."

Nevertheless, he said, "we still may have to wait a decade longer to make sure."

The British groups, headed by Phil Jones at East Anglia and David Parker of the meteorological office, reported 1990 to be the warmest year since comparable records were first kept in 1850.

"Although it is still too early to confirm whether the recent exceptional warmth is related to the greenhouse effect," the British scientists said in a statement, "international scientific opinion strongly supports the reality of this enhanced greenhouse effect, and it is likely that it has played some role in contributing to the recent warmth."

SATELLITES MEASURE WARMTH

A fourth analysis, of data from satellite measurements of the entire lower atmosphere through the first 11 months of 1990, showed the year could turn out to be the fourth warmest since the satellite measurements began in 1979. The analysis was made by John R. Christy of the University of Alabama and Roy Spencer of the space agency's Marshall Space Flight Center, both in Huntsville.

The Goddard group found that the record average surface temperature for the globe was eight-tenths of a degree Fahrenheit above the 1951-1980 average of 59 degrees. The British group found it seventh-tenths of a degree higher than the 1951-80 average.

The warming was particularly pronounced over the eastern United States, where record temperatures were also set in 1990, and across the entire Eurasian land mass, the Goddard team discovered. The only region with temperatures substantially below normal was Greenland and the neighboring Canadian archipelago. The British group found the warmth of 1990 "particularly evident" over Europe, western Siberia, the Far East and most of the United States and southern Canada.

The Federal Government reported last week that 1990 was the seventh warmest year in the United States since record-keeping began in 1895. In New York City, it was the warmest year recorded since the Government began measuring the temperature in Central Park in 1869.

Dr. Hansen's group calculated that the 1980's were about one degree warmer, globally, than the 1880's, and that 1990 was about 1.25 degrees warmer. By way of comparison, the world's average temperature is about 9 degrees warmer now than it was in the last ice age. Dr. Hansen said that the figures were corrected to take account of the "urban heat island effect," in which the growth of cities have caused land masses to warm by about about two-tenths of a degree.

The Goddard analysis also found that the rate of global warming for the past quarter-century was greater than at any other time since 1880. Scientists believe that natural climatic variation may have produced higher global temperatures at other junctures since the last ice age, but they have no reliable way of making comparisons between then and now.

Dr. Hansen said that if the global climate rises only about another two-tenths of a degree and remains there, the odds of warmer than normal winters and summers will increase substantially, and that this will be readily noticeable. "Seasonal temperature is still a crapshoot," he said, "but the global warming is loading the dice."

He calculates that with the two-tenths of a degree further warming, the chances for a warmer than normal season will increase from 1 in 3 to 2 in 3 and that the chances for a normal or colder than normal season decrease from 2 in 6 to 1 in 6.

"We're already close to there," he said.

While many scientists say it is not possible to conclude that the warming is being caused by increased greenhouse gases emitted as a result of human activity, Dr. Hansen said that the temperature increase "is roughly on the track" of what is predicted by computer models of the climate that try to predict the course of a greenhouse warming.

An international group of scientists convened under United Nations auspices found last year that if greenhouse gases continued to be emitted at the current rate, the earth's temperature would increase by about 2 degrees by the year 2025 and by more than 5 degrees by the end of the next century.

Given that range, scientists cannot say whether the warming would be mild or catastrophic, or which regions of the earth might be most affected.

A group of 16 Senators led by Al Gore, Democrat of Tennessee, yesterday signed a letter to President Bush citing the findings and saying that the data "illustrates clearly that global climate change is real, that global warming is not a problem that will disappear if we ignore it and that there is an increasingly urgent need for policies that address these issues."

Pro-Coal Ad Campaign Disputes Warming Idea

BY MATTHEW L. WALD | JULY 7, 1991

COAL-BURNING utility companies and coal producers, disturbed by public acceptance of the idea that burning fossil fuels will change the climate, are deciding whether to go national this fall with an ad campaign they tried in three markets earlier this year.

The advertising effort was tried out in Flagstaff, Ariz.; Fargo, N.D., and Bowling Green, Ky. The campaign produced nearly 2,000 requests to a toll-free telephone line for more information, said Gale Klappa, a vice president of the Southern Company, a coal-using utility based in Atlanta.

The goal of the campaign, according to one planning document, is to "reposition global warming as theory" and not fact.

In Bowling Green, an ad showed a cartoon horse in earmuffs and scarf and said, "If the Earth is getting warmer, why is Kentucky getting colder?" Another, with a cartoon man bundled up and holding a snow shovel, appeared in Minnesota and substituted "Minneapolis" for "Kentucky."

'ANOTHER VIEWPOINT'

"Those who are predicting catastrophe have been very effective at getting their message across in national media, and in so-called 'public service' announcements," Mr. Klappa said in a telephone interview. "But there is another viewpoint, a substantial viewpoint from a body of reputable scientists, and that viewpoint has really not been made available to a large majority."

A packet of internal correspondence and other information relating to the campaign was provided to The New York Times by the Sierra Club, the San Francisco-based environmental group that favors taking steps to reduce the risk of global warming. The organization had apparently been given the materials by someone who disagreed with the campaign's goals or approach.

Many climatologists are alarmed by the rising concentration in the Earth's atmosphere of carbon dioxide and other gases that they say will trap the sun's heat, raise temperatures and change rainfall patterns around the world. But scientists differ as to the extent of climate change or the speed with which it will occur.

MORE PUNCH WANTED

The three scientists who form a "science advisory panel" for the campaign said in telephone interviews that the salient element in two of the ads, that some areas might be getting cooler, did not contradict the theory of global warming. But one of the three, Robert C. Balling Jr., director of the office of Climatology at Arizona State University, said in a telephone interview that the advertising campaign designers felt that an ad that simply discussed the contradictory state of evidence for global warming would not have enough punch.

Dr. Balling and another member of the panel, Dr. Patrick J. Michaels, Virginia's climatologist and a professor of environmental sciences at the University of Virginia, have both asked to have their names removed from future mailings. Dr. Balling, who taped radio ads used in Flagstaff, said some people who heard the ads "did not like the idea that I was coming on the radio" and acting as "a mouthpiece" for a private group.

Dr. Michaels said that with only three names on the mailing, people would identify him as the source of the information, while he was not, in fact, the author, and that the size of the panel was so small that it made the position appear scientifically unpopular.

The third scientist on the panel, Dr. Sherwood B. Idso, an adjunct professor of botany and geography at Arizona State, said it was not clear whether adding carbon dioxide to the atmosphere would result in global warming or cooling, but that it would probably be beneficial because it would increase plant growth.

A scientist not affiliated with the campaign, Dr. John W. Firor, a climatologist at the National Oceanic and Atmospheric Administration's National Center for Atmospheric Research, in Boulder, Colo., said in an interview that pointing out that a single location ran against the predicted trend was "a straw man."

NAME SEARCH

Preparing for the test campaign, the organizers commissioned opinion surveys by Cambridge Reports, the Massachussetts research organization, to explore public attitudes toward global warming. Among the issues explored by Cambridge Reports was a name for the group, to conform with the acronym "ICE."

A Cambridge Reports document in the packet advised the group to adopt Information Council on the Environment rather than Informed Citizens for the Environment, because the latter name was "perceived as combining the attributes of activist and technical sources."

Cambridge Reports also suggested strategies like telling people that "some members of the media scare the public about global warming to increase their audience and their influence," according to documents in the packet.

The survey also showed, said the consultants, that "members of the public feel more comfortable expressing opinions on others' motivations and tactics than they do expressing opinions on scientific issues."

Mr. Klappa said in an interview that the advice was unsolicited and had not been followed.

DIVISION AMONG UTILITIES

The utility industry is divided on the question of global warming. Two California utilities, Southern California Edison, the nation's second-largest utility after the Pacific Gas and Electric Company, and the Los Angeles Water and Power Department, the largest municipal company, volunteered in May to cut their carbon-dioxide emissions by 20 percent in the next 20 years. Most of the savings, they said, would come from efficiency improvements in lighting, motors and cooling that would pay for themselves.

The Arizona Public Service Company, which serves Flagstaff, declined an invitation to participate in ICE. Mark De Michele, president and chief executive, did not reply to repeated phone calls seeking comment. But he told The Arizona Daily Sun in May, "The subject matter is far too complex and could be far more severe than the ads make of it for the subject to be dealt with in a slick ad campaign."

The Edison Electric Institute, a utility trade group based in Washington that also helped organize the ICE campaign, takes the position that because of the possibility that climate change is a real threat, steps should be taken to cut carbon-dioxide output if those steps are justifiable for other reasons — for example, saving money through higher efficiency or reducing the output of sulfur dioxide from power plants. That chemical causes acid rain.

Global Warming Experts Call Human Role Likely

BY WILLIAM K. STEVENS | SEPT. 9, 1995

IN AN IMPORTANT SHIFT of scientific judgment, experts advising the world's governments on climate change are saying for the first time that human activity is a likely cause of the warming of the global atmosphere.

While many climatologists have thought this to be the case, all but a few have held until now that the climate is so naturally variable that they could not be sure they were seeing a clear signal of the feared greenhouse effect — the heating of the atmosphere because of the carbon dioxide released by burning coal, oil and wood.

Even the string of very warm years in the 1980's and 1990's could have been just a natural swing of the climatic pendulum, the experts have said.

But a growing body of data and analysis now suggests that the warming of the last century, and especially of the last few years, "is unlikely to be entirely due to natural causes and that a pattern of climatic response to human activities is identifiable in the climatological record," says a draft summary of a new report by the Intergovernmental Panel on Climate Change.

The panel's role is to advise governments now negotiating reductions in emissions of greenhouse gases like carbon dioxide under the 1992 treaty on climate change.

The panel's draft summary, although intended for internal use, was recently made available on the Internet. The draft has been through at least one round of scientific review but its wording may change, since it is now being reviewed by governments. Scientists who prepared the full chapter on which the summary statement is based say they do not expect any substantial change in their basic assessment. The chapter has gone through extensive review by scientists around the world.

"I think the scientific justification for the statement is there, unequivocally," said Dr. Tom M. L. Wigley, a climatologist at the National Center for Atmospheric Research in Boulder, Colo., one of the chapter's authors.

The scientific community "has discovered the smoking gun," said Dr. Michael Oppenheimer, an atmospheric scientist with the Environmental Defense Fund, who is familiar with the draft report. "This finding is of paramount importance. For many years, policy makers have asked, 'Where's the signal?'" The intergovernmental panel, he said, "is telling us that the signal is here."

But Dr. Wigley and others involved in the reassessment say it is not yet known how much of the last century's warming can be attributed to human activity and how much is part of the earth's natural fluctuation that leads to ice ages at one extreme and warm periods at the other.

Nevertheless, the panel's conclusion marks a watershed in the views of climatologists, who with the notable exception of Dr. James E. Hansen of the NASA Goddard Institute for Space Studies in New York have until now refused to declare publicly that they can discern the signature of the greenhouse effect.

The new consensus, as represented by the intergovernmental panel, seems likely to stimulate more public debate over how seriously the threat of climate change should be taken.

As for the future, the draft summary forecasts an increase in the average global temperature of 1.44 degrees to 6.3 degrees Fahrenheit by the year 2100 if there is no further action to curb emissions of greenhouse gases. But that represents only 50 to 70 percent of the eventual warming, it says. These changes would be more rapid than any in the last 10,000 years, the period in which civilization developed, the panel says.

And it says that whatever action is taken in the future, the world still faces a further average temperature increase of 1 to 3.6 degrees.

By comparison, according to varying estimates, the average global temperature is 5 to 9 degrees warmer now than in the last ice age.

While a warmer world could be beneficial in some ways, the draft says, there would be many adverse effects. These include more extreme weather and possibly more intense tropical storms, destruction of some communities by rising seas, damage to and loss of natural ecosystems that cannot adapt rapidly enough, diminished agricultural output in some places and an increase in some tropical diseases.

Experts agree that the average surface temperature of the globe has already risen about 1 degree Fahrenheit in the last century, but there has long been debate over the cause.

Much of the argument has involved the computerized models of the atmosphere that have been climatologists' main tools in analyzing the warming problem. The models have many imperfections, but the panel scientists say they have improved and are being used more effectively.

Scientists say that a major reason for the change in view marked by the new report, in fact, is that a new generation of studies has enhanced their confidence in computer simulations of the atmosphere, creating a much better agreement between predicted patterns of climate change and those actually observed.

One study in particular, led by Dr. Benjamin B. Santer of the Lawrence Livermore National Laboratory, found a good match between the temperature differences from region to region predicted by computerized simulations of the atmosphere's response to increased carbon dioxide and those actually measured.

Dr. Santer is also an author of the intergovernmental panel's chapter on causes of the warming, along with Dr. Wigley, Dr. Tim P. Barnett of the Scripps Institution of Oceanography at La Jolla., Calif., and Dr. Ebby Anyamba, a Kenyan scientist currently at the NASA Goddard Space Flight Center in Greenbelt, Md. Twenty-seven other scientists contributed to the chapter.

The new generation of computer modeling studies employs more detailed and sophisticated representations of the atmosphere than when the intergovernmental panel made its first assessment of the climate problem in 1990. Scientists' confidence in the results of the comparisons between model predictions and observations has been boosted by more powerful statistical techniques used to validate the comparison between model predictions and observations, Dr. Wigley said.

Despite the new consensus among panel scientists, some skeptics, like Dr. Richard S. Lindzen of the Massachusetts Institute of Technology, remain unconvinced.

Dr. Lindzen said the panel's identification of the greenhouse signal "depends on the model estimate of natural variability being correct" — that is, the natural variability of the climate system on time scales of decades and centuries. The computer models do not reflect this well, he said, and therefore there is "no basis" yet for saying that a human influence on the climate has been detected.

Political views on climate change are considerably more diverse than those of the panel experts. Negotiations to reduce carbon dioxide emissions have been going on since they were begun in April by the parties to the climate treaty, but they are inching along. One reason has been the lack of scientific proof that human activities are responsible for the warming.

The Clinton Administration supports some reductions, while not specifying what kind or how much. But the ascendancy of conservatives in Congress has strengthened the hand of those who oppose reductions, mainly the fossil-fuel and related industries.

Meeting Reaches Accord to Reduce Greenhouse Gases

BY WILLIAM K. STEVENS | DEC. 11, 1997

NEGOTIATORS FROM around the world agreed today on a package of measures that for the first time would legally obligate industrial countries to cut emissions of waste industrial gases that scientists say are warming the earth's atmosphere.

But details on one contentious issue — the possible trade or sale of emission permits between countries — remain unsettled, and may remain unsettled for months, and the United States has said it wants this issue resolved before it signs the treaty. Any treaty is subject to approval by the United States Senate.

The agreement reached by delegates from more than 150 nations creates a landmark environmental policy to deal with global warming, and innovative new mechanisms to carry it out.

The nations would have a year to ratify the treaty, starting next March. Talks on "trading" of emissions are expected to take place next November.

Despite the uncertainties, some environmentalists hailed the agreement as a remarkable political and economic innovation, in that it would establish a global system for dealing with what many scientists believe is the overarching environmental concern.

Opponents of the treaty condemned it as economically ruinous.

The accord — known as the Kyoto Protocol — would require the industrial nations to reduce their emissions of carbon dioxide and five other heat-trapping greenhouse gases to 5.2 percent below those of 1990. The United States would be required to cut emissions 7 percent below 1990 levels, on average, in the years from 2008 through 2012.

The agreement appears to represent a significant concession by the United States, which previously had insisted on the less stringent course of reducing the emissions to 1990 levels, not below them. It is also a measure of the flexibility in the American bargaining position that Vice President Al Gore said he had ordered negotiators to adopt on a visit here Monday.

It remains to be seen, however, whether the White House can persuade the Senate to accept the agreement, or even whether the United States will sign it.

Many Senators had already expressed reservations about the less stringent Administration proposal. By 2000, emissions of greenhouse gases by the United States are expected to be about 13 percent higher than they were in 1990. They are expected to be perhaps 30 percent higher in 2010, if trends in energy use continue and no other action is taken.

Senator Chuck Hagel, a Nebraska Republican observing the talks, said here today, "Any way you measure this, this is a very bad deal for America." He predicted the Senate would not approve it.

For his part Stuart Eizenstat, the senior American negotiator, said the United States was still waiting for more signs of flexibility from developing nations on the question of emission trading.

"We do not yet have that meaningful commitment coming out of Kyoto," he said. But, he added, the possibilities for such a commitment "are certainly pregnant."

President Clinton, visiting New York, said in a statement that he was "very pleased" by the agreement, which he said was "environmentally strong and economically sound." But he said developing nations had to do more.

And in Washington, Vice President Gore called the agreement a "vital turning point." He added, "Clearly, more work is needed. In particular we will continue to press for meaningful participation by key developing nations. We are confident that can be achieved."

Under the accord, different countries would be assigned different targets, depending on their national circumstances and economic profiles. The European Union's target was set at a reduction in emissions of 8 percent below 1990 levels, and that of Japan at 6 percent. Other targets, albeit within a narrow range, also applied to other developed countries. Some countries may be allowed to increase emissions, but globally, emissions are to be reduced by 30 percent from the levels currently projected for 2010.

After an all-night session that ran into an unscheduled 11th day of discussion, the protocol was approved by representatives of more than 150 countries.

The countries were modifying an agreement, negotiated in Rio de Janeiro in 1992, that called for voluntary efforts to limit emission of greenhouse gases. The burning of fossil fuels like coal and oil is responsible for most emissions of carbon dioxide, the most important greenhouse gas.

As a means of promoting reductions in developing countries, the delegates established a special mechanism for transferring energy-efficient technologies and nonpolluting forms of energy production from richer nations to poorer ones. Greater efficiency means fewer emissions, and alternative energy sources like solar and wind power mean none.

The Clean Development Mechanism, as the new arrangement was named, is intended to encourage companies in industrial countries to invest in emissions-reduction projects in developing countries — modern, fuel-efficient power plants, for example — and get some credit for reducing their own emissions.

But the agreement was held up for hours last night and this morning by the resistance of some developing countries, including China, India and Saudi Arabia, to the inclusion of a provision enabling the industrialized nations to trade or purchase emissions rights. The United States considers this arrangement the cheapest and most efficient way of cutting emissions. Without it, American negotiators said, it would be impossible for the country to meet its emission targets.

In emissions trading, a country or industrial company will be able to meet its emissions reduction target by cutting some of its emissions itself, while at the same time purchasing part of its required reduction from another country or company that achieved excess cuts.

Based on its success with trading emissions of sulfur dioxide, a chemical implicated in acid rain, the United States argues that larger and cheaper reductions can be achieved with this mechanism.

The objectors said that the mechanism could lead to shifting the burden to less developed countries, and that countries and companies might be able to buy their way out of their obligations.

After hours of argument, delegates agreed to allow the parties to the 1992 treaty to postpone negotiations on the principles, rules, guidelines and operations of the trading system until November.

Experts advising the negotiators here say that if emissions are not reduced, the average surface temperature of the globe will rise by 2 to 6 degrees Fahrenheit over the next century, causing widespread climatic, environmental and economic disruption.

Philip E. Clapp, president of the the National Environmental Trust in Washington, who has been observing the talks here, called the agreement "a historic landmark in environmental protection." He said it would be remembered "as a central achievement of the Clinton-Gore Administration."

But representatives of the American fossil fuel and heavy manufacturing industries saw disaster in the agreement.

"It is a terrible deal and the President should not sign it," said William K. O'Keefe, chairman of the Global Climate Coalition, an industry group. Mr. O'Keefe said that "business, labor and agriculture will campaign hard and will defeat" the treaty if it is submitted to the Senate for ratification.

The protocol is generally viewed only as an early step in a continuing attempt to deal with the question of climate change. It is generally acknowledged that any attempt to deal with the problem requires a global solution involving all countries.

Industrial Group Plans
to Battle Climate Treaty

BY JOHN H. CUSHMAN JR. | APRIL 26, 1998

INDUSTRY OPPONENTS of a treaty to fight global warming have drafted an ambitious proposal to spend millions of dollars to convince the public that the environmental accord is based on shaky science.

Among their ideas is a campaign to recruit a cadre of scientists who share the industry's views of climate science and to train them in public relations so they can help convince journalists, politicians and the public that the risk of global warming is too uncertain to justify controls on greenhouse gases like carbon dioxide that trap the sun's heat near Earth.

An informal group of people working for big oil companies, trade associations and conservative policy research organizations that oppose the treaty have been meeting recently at the Washington office of the American Petroleum Institute to put the plan together.

Joe Walker, a public relations representative of the petroleum institute who is leading the project, said in an interview that the plan had been under consideration for about two months and was "very, very tentative." Mr. Walker said no industry executives had yet been approached to pay for it.

But an eight-page memorandum that he wrote shows in detail how some industry lobbyists are going about opposing the climate treaty.

It is a daunting public relations task. Whenever the treaty's advocates, including the Clinton Administration, discuss global warming, they present the science as essentially settled and unchallengeable, and they compare dissenting scientists to discredited apologists for the tobacco companies. That view has become widely accepted among reporters and the public.

Although mainstream scientists do identify considerable uncertainties in their climate predictions, which are based on computer models, they are increasingly confident that global warming is a serious problem and often say that the uncertainties do not justify inaction.

Based on the latest science, most of the world's nations agreed in Rio de Janeiro in 1992 that industrial nations should cut emissions of greenhouse gases, and the treaty was modified last year to require further reductions in emissions to levels well below those of 1990, over the next 10 to 15 years. But the United States Senate has not yet agreed to that treaty provision, which could require deep reductions in American consumption of fossil fuels.

Documents describing the proposal to undermine the mainstream view were given to The New York Times by the National Environmental Trust, whose work in support of the global-warming treaty is financed by philanthropic organizations, including the Pew Charitable Trusts, the biggest of the nation's pro-environment grant makers.

Phil Clapp, the president of the environmental trust, said he obtained the papers from an industry official. Exposing the plan at this stage, Mr. Clapp said, would probably ruin the effort to raise money to carry out the plan.

Industry representatives confirmed that the documents were authentic, but emphasized that the plans had not been formally approved by participating organizations. The document listed representatives of the Exxon Corporation, the Chevron Corporation and the Southern Company as being involved. Representatives of Chevron and Southern acknowledged attending meetings on the project; the Exxon representative could not be reached for comment.

The draft plan calls for recruiting scientists to argue against the Administration, and suggests that they include "individuals who do not have a long history of visibility and/or participation in the climate change debate."

But among the plan's advocates are groups already linked to the best-known critics of global-warming science.

They include the Science and Environment Policy Project, founded by Fred Singer, a physicist noted for opposing the mainstream view of climate science. Frederick Seitz, another prominent skeptic on global warming, is involved with two other groups mentioned in the plan: the George C. Marshall Institute, where Dr. Seitz is chairman, and the Advancement of Sound Science Coalition, where he is on the science advisory board.

On Monday, the National Academy of Sciences disassociated itself from the most recent effort to drum up support among skeptical scientists. That effort came in the form of a statement and petition on global warming circulated by Dr. Seitz, a physicist who was president of the academy in the 1960's.

The petition, attacking the scientific conclusions underlying the treaty on climate change, was accompanied by an article that was formatted to resemble one that might have been published in the academy's prestigious peer-reviewed journal. It was not.

The draft plan, recently discussed at the oil industry offices, calls for giving such dissenters on climate science "the logistical and moral support they have been lacking."

It also calls for spending $5 million over two years to "maximize the impact of scientific views consistent with ours on Congress, the media and other key audiences."

It would measure progress by counting, among other things, the percentage of news articles that raise questions about climate science and the number of radio talk show appearances by scientists questioning the prevailing views.

The document says that industry's polling, conducted by Charlton Research, has found that while Americans see climate change as a serious threat, "public opinion is open to change on climate science."

Supporters of the plan want to raise money quickly to spend much of it between now and the November negotiating session in Buenos Aires, where important details of the international treaty are to be decided.

A proposed media-relations budget of $600,000, not counting any money for advertising, would be directed at science writers, editors, columnists and television network correspondents, using as many as 20 "respected climate scientists" recruited expressly "to inject credible science and scientific accountability into the global climate debate, thereby raising questions about and undercutting the 'prevailing scientific wisdom.'"

Among the tasks, the petroleum institute's memorandum said, would be to "identify, recruit and train a team of five independent scientists to participate in media outreach."

What the industry group wanted to provide, the memorandum said, was "a one-stop resource on climate science for members of Congress, the media, industry and all others concerned."

The industry group said it wanted to develop "a sound scientific alternative" to the Intergovernmental Panel on Climate Change, a large group of scientists advising the United Nations that has published the most authoritative scientific assessments of global warming. That panel has predicted that the next century will bring widespread climatic disruptions if actions are not taken to reverse the accumulation of greenhouse gases in the atmosphere.

The draft plan suggests that despite industry efforts to convince the public that the climate treaty would be costly to carry out and unfair to the United States, the treaty remains popular partly because environmentalists are winning the debate on the science.

"Indeed, the public has been highly receptive to the Clinton Administration's plans," the memorandum said. "There has been little, if any, public resistance or pressure applied to Congress to reject the treaty, except by those 'inside the Beltway' with vested interests."

CHAPTER 5

Reality Sinks In: The 2000s

The scientific community agreed that the evidence of human-caused global climate change is incontrovertible. Climate experts issued more stringent warnings about the dangers of global warming. And former Vice President Al Gore produced a documentary that drove the message home. People began to demand state, federal, and international action to help prevent disaster, and politicians began new talks about climate treaties.

A Shift in Stance on Global Warming Theory

BY ANDREW C. REVKIN | OCT. 25, 2000

GREENHOUSE GASES produced mainly by the burning of fossil fuels are altering the atmosphere in ways that affect earth's climate, and it is likely that they have "contributed substantially to the observed warming over the last 50 years," an international panel of climate scientists has concluded. The panel said temperatures could go higher than previously predicted if emissions are not curtailed.

This represents a significant shift in tone — from couched to relatively confident — for the panel of hundreds of scientists, the Intergovernmental Panel on Climate Change, which issued two previous assessments of the research into global warming theory, in 1995 and 1990.

The conclusions are likely to resonate loudly next month when negotiators from most of the world's nations gather in The Hague to work out details of the Kyoto Protocol, a treaty intended to cut releases of carbon dioxide and other greenhouse gases. The 1997 treaty has been signed by more than 150 countries but has not yet been ratified by any industrialized country.

The panel, which operates under the auspices of the World Meteorological Organization and the United Nations Environment Program, is spelling out its new findings in a climate assessment it began working on three years ago and which fills 1,000 pages. A summary of its findings was sent this week to governments around the world for a last round of comments before the assessment is completed at a meeting in January in Shanghai. Given the significance of issue and the disagreements over how to deal with it, there are likely to be changes before the summary and the 14 chapters of research underlying it go to print sometime next year, several scientists involved in the project said.

A copy of the summary was obtained by The New York Times from someone who was eager to have the findings disseminated before the meetings in The Hague.

Many panel members said that the summary represents the closest thing to a consensus possible in science, which is generally driven more by questioning and challenges than by esprit de corps.

In interviews, several members of the panel declined to discuss details of the report or the summary, saying they were not yet in their final form. But they said recent advances in the study of climate change led them to see with greater clarity the role of people in climate change.

For example, they pointed to additional temperature data gathered in the last few years, which have been substantially warmer than any similar string of years in many centuries; to improvements in computer models designed to project future trends; and to better understanding of the influence of other climate-influencing emissions, like particles of sulfates that can cool the earth by reflecting sunlight back into space.

Meanwhile, they said in interviews and in the summary, evidence of increasing warming has shown up in retreating glaciers, thinning polar sea ice, retreating snow packs, warmer nights, and elsewhere.

"More and more people working in atmospheric science or on climate or ecology have had to come to grips with the fact that climate change is affecting what they're looking at," said Dr. Kevin E. Trenberth, the head of the climate analysis division of the National Center for Atmospheric Research in Boulder, Colo., and a lead author of the panel's summary. "There is increasing evidence from many sources that the signal of human influence on climate has emerged from natural variability, sometime around 1980."

The report's language is far more constrained than that, reflecting a delicate consensus that was reached only after months of debate and several rounds of comments by hundreds of scientists and government climate experts, Dr. Trenberth said.

One of its most striking findings is its conclusion that the upper range of warming over the next 100 years could be even higher than it estimated in 1995, in a worst case raising the average global temperature 11 degrees Fahrenheit from where it was in 1990. By comparison, average temperatures today are only 9 degrees Fahrenheit warmer than they were at the end of the last Ice Age.

In its 1995 analysis, the panel concluded that a worst case would raise temperatures 6.3 degrees. The worsening of the picture, ironically, is due to a projected cleansing of the atmosphere in coming decades of other emissions from fuel burning that have a cooling influence on climate — specifically the veil of tiny particles of sulfates from unfiltered burning of coal and oil that contribute to smog and acid rain.

In the last century, these sun-blocking particles probably masked substantial warming, scientists say. If they are increasingly removed as more smokestacks and tailpipes are filtered around the world, the warming from carbon dioxide and other greenhouse gases would not be counteracted, the report concludes.

Not everyone is satisfied with the document or the process that produced it. Dr. Richard S. Lindzen, a climate expert at the Massachusetts Institute of Technology who has been a prominent dissenter from the view that human activity is altering climate, helped write one chapter of the assessment but is skeptical about the importance of the human contribution to any future warming.

He described the summary as "waffle words designed for one thing, to ensure that the issue remains important enough that it not be put on a back burner."

Over all, he said, there is little solid evidence that any climate change would have harmful effects.

Still, even Dr. Lindzen said that he felt that the human influence on the earth's climate is now established.

"There has to be a human component to the change that's under way," he said.

The summary itself acknowledged the need for much more research, but also laid out many potentially dire consequences if the warming even takes a middle course. Even if emissions of carbon dioxide and the other gases are sharply reduced, it said, "sea level will continue to rise due to thermal expansion for hundreds of years."

Dr. Michael Oppenheimer, a climate scientist at Environmental Defense, a private environmental group and one of the authors of the summary, said it represented a balanced, sober assessment of the risks ahead.

Other scientists involved in the assessment pointed out that the authors of the summary also included Dr. Mack McFarland, an atmospheric scientist at a division of DuPont, and several other experts approaching the question from the point of view of industry.

Together, they concluded that the nuanced language of 1995, which said "the balance of evidence suggests a discernible human influence on global climate," was clearly out of date.

178 Nations Reach a Climate Accord. U.S. Only Looks On.

BY ANDREW C. REVKIN | JULY 24, 2001

WITH THE BUSH ADMINISTRATION on the sidelines, the world's leading countries hammered out a compromise agreement today finishing a treaty that for the first time would formally require industrialized countries to cut emissions of gases linked to global warming.

The agreement, which was announced here today after three days of marathon bargaining, rescued the Kyoto Protocol, the preliminary accord framed in Japan in 1997, that was the first step toward requiring cuts in such gases. That agreement has been repudiated by President Bush, who has called it fatally flawed," saying it places too much of the cleanup burden on industrial countries and would be too costly to the American economy.

Today, his national security adviser, Condoleezza Rice, said in Rome, where the president met with the pope, "I don't believe that it is a surprise to anyone that the United States believes that this particular protocol is not in its interests, nor do we believe that it really addresses the problem of global climate change." She reiterated that the president had created a task force to come up with alternatives.

The agreement by 178 countries was largely the product of give and take involving Japan, Australia, Canada and the European Union. But Japan's role was crucial because it is the largest economy after the United States and its opposition would have killed any agreement.

Largely as a result of concessions to Japan, the product is a significantly softened version of the Kyoto accord, allowing industrial nations with the greatest emissions of greenhouse gases, principally carbon dioxide, to achieve their cuts with greater flexibility. For example, Japan won a provision to receive credits for reducing the gases by protecting forests that absorb carbon dioxide.

Still, the agreement is a binding contract among nations — excluding the United States — under which 38 industrialized countries must reduce those emissions by 2012 or face tougher emissions goals. Those countries now account for close to half of the emissions. The agreement now moves to a complex ratification process that calls for approval from the biggest polluting countries, which can be achieved even with United States opposition.

Officials from the European Union exulted over the compromise. Olivier Deleuze, the energy and sustainability secretary of Belgium, said there were easily 10 things in the final texts that he could criticize. "But," he said, "I prefer an imperfect agreement that is living than a perfect agreement that doesn't exist."

The Kyoto accord calls for the 38 industrialized countries by 2012 to reduce their combined annual gas emissions to 5.2 percent below levels measured in 1990. It set a different, negotiated target for each, with Japan, for example, accepting a target of cutting gas emissions back to 6 percent below 1990 emissions. Those targets were included in the Kyoto agreement and were untouched by the compromise today. Developing countries do not have to do anything to reduce emissions.

The biggest sticking point was how much to penalize countries that miss their targets. Japan held out for a fairly painless system. Europe wanted countries that missed targets in the first commitment period, from 2008 to 2012, to pledge to reduce more carbon dioxide in the next period, with the equivalent of penalties plus interest.

On that point, Europe got its way.

The talks also clarified the design of the first global system for buying and selling credits earned by reducing carbon dioxide emissions. Such a system tends to focus investment in pollution cleanups where the job can be done effectively and cheaply.

In general, Japan was in the driver's seat. After Mr. Bush rejected the treaty, Japan became a pivotal player. It sought, and received, extra credits toward its emissions goals for protecting its forests.

Forest experts calculated that the credits for forests essentially would drop Japan's target from 6 percent below 1990 levels to just 2 percent below. Canada and Russia would gain large forest credits as well.

But climate scientists said that in most cases the forest credits were not as big a gift as they seemed, and that economic growth — if continued as projected — would put all the industrialized countries listed under the treaty 15 or 20 percent above their 1990 levels. So a drop even close to 1990 figures would be a big change, they said, essentially lessening the benefit of the forest credits.

Still, some participants grumbled about countries getting credit for gas reductions "by watching trees grow," as one environmentalist put it. The compromise was laced with of something for just about everyone.

The European Union pledged $410 million a year through the first years of the treaty to help developing countries adapt to climate change and build the technological ability to avoid adding to the problem.

That was something demanded by, among others, Saudi Arabia, among the group of developing countries that are not required to reduce their emissions.

The difficulties in moving ahead on the Kyoto Protocol far exceeded those surrounding other environmental treaties, experts said, because the treaty, by controlling carbon dioxide, the main greenhouse gas, would limit something released by almost every act of daily living.

That this was an economic as well as environmental treaty was evident at every turn.

"This protocol is about the climate, but it is also about the interests of each country," explained Ali Al-Naimi, the Saudi oil minister.

Indeed, he said, Saudi Arabia's interest lay not so much in curtailing gases, but in preventing economic disruption should the treaty lead the world to curtail its use of oil.

Much of the momentum appeared to be maintained personally by Jan Pronk, the indefatigable Dutch environment minister and chairman of the talks here. Mr. Pronk often locked himself in a room with clusters of delegates. By dawn today, dozens of delegates were sprawled asleep on every spare cushion and couch in the meeting rooms of the Maritim Hotel.

In the end, the diverse array of countries at the table, faced with the possibility of an embarrassing collapse of the entire treaty, overcame their differences.

The compromise caps a six-year struggle between a group of industries and countries that claimed mandatory emissions caps would harm economies, and environmental groups and other nations that saw such limits as the only way to stave off potentially disruptive climate shifts.

At the meeting, there were unusual combinations of interests, with companies that build nuclear power plants eager to jump into the climate fight because nuclear power produces electricity without emitting greenhouse gases. Japan, Canada, China and other countries supported credits toward emission targets by substituting nuclear power.

But the European Union, despite wide use of nuclear power in some large European countries, insisted there be no nuclear option in the agreement.

To some of the participants here, the achievement was a bit hollow given that the United States, which by some measurements accounts for about 25 percent of greenhouse gases, chose not to participate.

Others noted that, among them, the three dozen industrialized countries that supported the treaty language accounted for far more emissions than the United States.

Environmental campaigners said Europe had proved it could lead despite its sometimes fragmented appearance.

"There's really a new force on the world stage," said Philip Clapp, the president of the National Environmental Trust, a lobbying group based in Washington. "If the United States will not lead, Europe can and will."

Many of the negotiators from other countries held out hope that, eventually, the United States would rejoin the pact.

Chances of that happening in the short run are slim. During the session celebrating the accord, Paula Dobrianksy, the under secretary of state for global affairs, congratulated the parties to the protocol but reiterated a common theme of the Bush administration — that it was "not sound policy." She did not come to Bonn with any alternative ideas.

Japan's environment minister, Yoriko Kawaguchi, in a clear reference to the United States, said it was important to try to build a bridge between the Kyoto process and countries waiting on the sidelines.

"In order to achieve the objectives of the Kyoto Protocol, we need to have the widest possible participation of countries," Ms. Kawaguchi said. "We should try to encourage all our friends to join us in our common effort to address global warming."

Politics Reasserts Itself in the Debate Over Climate Change and Its Hazards

BY ANDREW C. REVKIN | AUG. 5, 2003

JUST AS THE GLOBAL CLIMATE ebbs and surges, with droughts followed by deluges, so does the politically charged atmosphere that has long surrounded research pointing to potentially disruptive global warming.

The political turbulence always seems to intensify when there is momentum toward actions to limit smokestack and tailpipe releases of carbon dioxide, the main heat-trapping greenhouse gas, which most experts link to rising temperatures.

Such a surge occurred last week. Scientists who have called for action and those who say risks from warming are overblown agree that it has been many years since research on warming has been the subject of such a vigorous assault.

The week started with an effort by Senator John McCain, Republican of Arizona, and Senator Joseph I. Lieberman, Democrat of Connecticut, to force a vote on their proposed bill requiring eventual limits on emissions of greenhouse gases.

Opponents of curbs on emissions responded with an intensive challenge to the broadening scientific consensus on global warming. Around the capital, there was a flurry of debates, Senate speeches, inflammatory editorials and talk-show commentaries, some contending that global warming was an alarmist fantasy and others saying action was essential.

In a two-hour speech on July 28 on the Senate floor, Senator James M. Inhofe, the Oklahoma Republican who is chairman of the Environment and Public Works Committee, said:

"With all of the hysteria, all of the fear, all of the phony science, could it be that man-made global warming is the greatest hoax ever perpetrated on the American people? It sure sounds like it."

Mr. Inhofe convened a hearing on Tuesday that focused on the work of the small core of researchers who insist that there is no evidence for human-caused warming of any import. A spokesman for Mr. Inhofe, Michael Catanzaro, defended the hearing, saying its goal was "to strip away political factors and just get to the hard science."

But both believers and skeptics said the events vividly illustrated how politics could contort science. Instead of the standard scientific process in which researchers sift disparate findings for common elements to build consensus, they say, partisans seem to be sifting only for the findings that fit their agendas.

Dr. Roger A. Pielke Jr., director of the Center for Science and Technology Policy Research at the University of Colorado, said the partisanship seemed to be spreading beyond officials and interest groups.

"On the climate issue, we appear to be on the brink of having Republican science and Democrat science," said Dr. Pielke, who has long espoused acting to limits risks from warming. "If so, then this simply arrays scientists on opposing sides of a gridlocked issue, when what we really need from scientists is new and practical alternatives that might depoliticize the issue."

Skeptics agreed that politics was invading the practice of climate science.

"Climate science is at its absolutely most political," said Dr. Patrick J. Michaels, a climatologist at the University of Virginia who, through an affiliation with the Cato Institute, a libertarian group in Washington, has criticized statements that global warming poses big dangers.

The Inhofe hearing aside, Dr. Michaels said, his fear is that minority scientific voices will eventually be squelched by mainstream views.

But many of the scientists who warn of dangers say the real risk arises from confusion that a handful of skeptical scientists has perpetuated. That prolongs the debate over how to respond, those scientists say.

Strangely, the fresh attacks on climate science have come even as some skeptics' projections on warming, including those of Dr. Michaels, have started to overlap with those of the dominant group of researchers.

Dr. Michaels, in a recent paper, projected that the global average temperature was most likely to rise about 3 degrees from 1990 to 2100. That is three times as much as the rise measured in the 20th century and within the mainstream projections that skeptical scientists had in years past criticized as alarmist.

The fight has evolved from clashing over human actions and whether they are warming the planet to portraying the consequences of warming as harmful, insignificant or even beneficial.

The last big peak in politics-tinged attacks over global warming came in 1997, when months of lobbying preceded international consensus on the Kyoto Protocol, the first treaty that required industrialized countries to reduce heat-trapping smokestack and tailpipe emissions.

That pact, though rejected by the Bush administration, has been embraced by almost all other big nations and needs only ratification by Russia to take effect.

After Mr. Inhofe's hearing, both sides quickly claimed victory, scoring the hearing like a sports event.

Republican strategists said the widely divergent views on global warming expressed by the three invited scientists — two longtime skeptics and one scientist who has built the case for concern — reinforced the idea that climate science was still split. That is a crucial goal of industries and officials who are fighting restrictions on emissions.

Advocates for cuts in emissions and scientists who hold the prevailing view on warming said the hearing backfired. It proved more convincingly, they said, that the skeptical scientists were a fringe element that had to rely increasingly on industry money and peripheral scientific journals to promote their work.

The hearing featured Dr. Willie Soon, an astrophysicist at the Harvard-Smithsonian Center for Astrophysics and a co-author of a study, with Dr. Sallie Baliunas, also an astrophysicist at the center, that said the 20th-century warming trend was unremarkable compared with other climate shifts over the last 1,000 years.

But the Soon-Baliunas paper, published in the journal Climate Research this year, has been heavily criticized by many scientists, including several of the journal editors. The editors said last week that whether or not the conclusions were correct, the analysis was deeply flawed.

The publisher of the journal, Dr. Otto Kinne, and an editor who recently became editor in chief, Dr. Hans von Storch, both said that in retrospect the paper should not have been published as written. Dr. Kinne defended the journal and its process of peer review, but distanced himself from the paper.

"I have not stood behind the paper by Soon and Baliunas," he wrote in an e-mail message. "Indeed: the reviewers failed to detect methodological flaws."

Dr. von Storch, who was not involved in overseeing the paper, resigned last week, saying he disagreed with the peer-review policies.

The Senate hearing also focused new scrutiny on Dr. Soon and Dr. Baliunas's and ties to advocacy groups. The scientists also receive income as senior scientists for the George C. Marshall Institute, a Washington group that has long fought limits on gas emissions. The study in Climate Research was in part underwritten by $53,000 from the American Petroleum Institute, the voice of the oil industry.

Critics of Mr. Inhofe noted that he said in his speech last week that his committee should consider only "the most objective science."

In an interview on Friday, Dr. Soon said he separated his affiliation with the advocacy groups from his research.

"I have my views on things," Dr. Soon said. "But as a scientist I'm really interested in what are the facts."

After such a raucous week, Dr. Soon seemed eager to return to the relatively quiet realm of academic debate. "We should all just try to resolve this issue," he said, "instead of going into a Senate hearing with all this circus."

The circus, however, promises to return to town. The Senate has agreed to vote on the McCain-Lieberman bill in the fall.

Bush vs. the Laureates: How Science Became a Partisan Issue

BY ANDREW C. REVKIN | OCT. 19, 2004

WHY IS SCIENCE seemingly at war with President Bush?

For nearly four years, and with rising intensity, scientists in and out of government have criticized the Bush administration, saying it has selected or suppressed research findings to suit preset policies, skewed advisory panels or ignored unwelcome advice, and quashed discussion within federal research agencies.

Administration officials see some of the criticism as partisan, and some perhaps a function of unrealistic expectations on the part of scientists about their role in policy debates. "This administration really does not like regulation and it believes in market processes in general," said Dr. John H. Marburger III, the president's science adviser, who is a Democrat.

"So there's always going to be a tilt in an administration like this one to a certain set of actions that you take to achieve some policy objective," he went on. "In general, science may give you some limits and tell you some boundary conditions on that set of actions, but it really doesn't tell you what to do."

Dr. Jesse H. Ausubel, an expert on energy and climate at Rockefeller University, said some of the bitterness expressed by other researchers could stem from their being excluded from policy circles that were open to them under previous administrations. "So these people who believe themselves important feel themselves belittled," he said.

Indeed, much of the criticism has come from private groups, like the Union of Concerned Scientists and many environmental organizations, with long records of opposing positions the administration favors.

Nevertheless, political action by scientists has not been so forceful since 1964, when Barry Goldwater's statements promoting the deployment of battlefield nuclear weapons spawned the creation of the 100,000-member group Scientists and Engineers for Johnson.

This year, 48 Nobel laureates dropped all pretense of nonpartisanship as they signed a letter endorsing Senator John Kerry. "Unlike previous administrations, Republican and Democratic alike, the Bush administration has ignored unbiased scientific advice in the policy making that is so important to our collective welfare," they wrote. The critics include members of past Republican administrations.

And battles continue to erupt in government agencies over how to communicate research findings that might clash with administration policies.

This month, three NASA scientists and several officials at NASA headquarters and at two agency research centers described how news releases on new global warming studies had been revised by administrators to play down definitiveness or risks. The scientists and officials said other releases had been delayed. "You have to be evenhanded in reporting science results, and it's apparent that there is a tendency for that not to be occurring now," said Dr. James E. Hansen, a climate expert who is director of the NASA Goddard Institute for Space Studies in Manhattan.

Glenn Mahone, the assistant administrator of NASA for public affairs, yesterday denied that any releases on climate had been held up or modified by anything other than normal reviews. "There has been a slowdown," he said.

But he insisted, "There is nothing in terms of any kind of approval process with the White House."

Earlier this year, after continuing complaints that the White House was asking litmus-test questions of nominees for scientific advisory panels, the first question asked of a candidate for a panel on Arctic issues, the candidate said, was: "Do you support the president?"

When asked about such incidents, officials with the Bush campaign call attention to Mr. Bush's frequent queries to the National Academy of Sciences as evidence of his desire for good advice on technical issues.

"This president believes in pursuing the best, most objective science, and his record proves that," said Brian Jones, a campaign spokesman.

Yet complaints about the administration's approach to scientific information are coming even from within the government. Many career scientists and officials have expressed frustration and anger privately but were unwilling to be identified for fear of losing their jobs. But a few have stepped forward, including Dr. Hansen at NASA, who has been researching global warming and conveying its implications to Congress and the White House for two decades.

Dr. Hansen, who was invited to brief the Bush cabinet twice on climate and whose work has been cited by Mr. Bush, said he had decided to speak publicly about the situation because he was convinced global warming posed a serious threat and that further delays in addressing it would add to the risks.

"It's something that I've been worrying about for months," he said, describing his decision. "If I don't do something now I'll regret it."

"Under the Clinton-Gore administration, you did have occasions when Al Gore knew the answer he wanted, and he got annoyed if you presented something that wasn't consistent with that," Dr. Hansen said. "I got a little fed up with him, but it was not institutionalized the way it is now."

Under the Bush administration, he said, "they're picking and choosing information according to the answer that they want to get, and they've appointed so many people who are just focused on this that they really are having an impact on the day-to-day flow of information."

Disputes between scientists and the administration have erupted over stem cell policy, population control and Iraq's nuclear weapons research. But nowhere has the clash been more intense or sustained than in the area of climate change.

There the intensity of the disagreements has been stoked not only by disputes over claimed distortion or suppression of research findings, but on the other side by the enormous economic implications.

Several dozen interviews with administration officials and with scientists in and out of government, along with a variety of documents, show that the core of the clash is over instances in which scientists say that objective and relevant information is ignored or distorted in service of pre-established policy goals. Scientists were essentially locked out of important internal White House debates; candidates for advisory panels were asked about their politics as well as their scientific work; and the White House exerted broad control over how scientific findings were to be presented in public reports or news releases.

AN EARLY SKIRMISH

Climate emerged as a prickly issue in the first months of Mr. Bush's term, when the White House began forging its energy policy and focusing on ways to increase domestic use of coal and production of oil.

In March 2001, a White House team used a single economic analysis by the Energy Department to build a case that Mr. Bush quickly used to back out of his campaign pledge to restrict power plant discharges of carbon dioxide, the main heat-trapping gas linked to global warming.

The analysis, from December 2000, was based on a number of assumptions, including one that no technological innovation would occur. The result showed that prompt cuts in carbon dioxide from power plants would weaken the economy.

Other analyses, including some by other branches of the Department of Energy, drew different conclusions but were ignored.

Advice from climate experts at the Environmental Protection Agency was sought but also ignored. A March 7 memorandum from agency experts to the White House team recommended that the carbon dioxide pledge be kept, saying the Energy Department study "was based on assumptions that do not apply" to Mr. Bush's plan and "inflates the costs of achieving carbon dioxide reductions." The memo was given to The New York Times by a former E.P.A. official who says science was not adequately considered.

Nonetheless, the White House team stuck to its course, drafting a memo on March 8 to John Bridgeland, the president's domestic policy adviser, that used the energy study to argue for abandoning the campaign promise.

None of the authors was a scientist. The team consisted of Cesar Conda, an adviser to Vice President Dick Cheney and now a political consultant; Andrew Lundquist, the White House energy policy director, who is now an energy lobbyist; Kyle E. McSlarrow, the chairman of Dan Quayle's 2000 presidential campaign and now deputy secretary of energy; Robert C. McNally Jr., an energy and economic analyst who is now an investment banker; Karen Knutson, a deputy on energy policy and a former Republican Senate aide; and Marcus Peacock, an analyst on science and energy issues from the Office of Management and Budget. They concluded that Mr. Bush could continue to say he believed that global warming was occurring but make a case that "any specific policy proposals or approaches aimed at addressing global warming must await further scientific inquiry."

A copy of the memo was recently given to The New York Times by a White House adviser at the time who now disagrees with the administration's chosen policies.

The Environmental Protection Agency tried one more time to argue that Mr. Bush should not change course.

In a section of a March 9 memo to the White House headed "Global warming science is compelling," agency officials said: "The science is strongest on the fact that carbon dioxide is contributing, and will continue to contribute, to global climate change. The greatest scientific uncertainties concern how fast the climate will change and what will be the regional impacts. Even within these bands of uncertainty, however, it is clear that global warming is an issue that must be addressed."

On March 13, Mr. Bush signed and sent a letter to four Republican senators who had sought clarification of the administration's climate plans. In it, Mr. Bush described the Energy Department study as "important new information that warrants a re-evaluation, especially at a time of rising energy prices and a serious energy shortage."

He said reconsideration of the carbon dioxide curbs was particularly appropriate "given the incomplete state of scientific knowledge of the causes of, and solutions to, global climate change."

The letter also reiterated his longstanding opposition to the Kyoto Protocol, the climate treaty now moving toward enactment in almost all other industrialized countries.

In the next months, the White House set up a series of briefings on climate science and economics for the cabinet and also sought the advice of the National Academy of Sciences. The experts convened by the academy reaffirmed the scientific consensus that recent warming has human causes and that significant risks lie ahead. But the administration's position on what to do has not changed.

HIDDEN ASSUMPTIONS

A handful of experts who have worked on climate policy in the Bush and Clinton administrations say that both tried to skew information to favor policies, but that there were distinct differences.

Andrew G. Keeler, who until June 2001 was on the president's Council of Economic Advisers and has since returned to teaching at the University of Georgia, said the Clinton administration had also played with economic calculations of the costs of curbing carbon dioxide emissions, in its case to show that limiting emissions would not be expensive.

But it made available all of the assumptions that went into its analysis, he said; by contrast, the Bush administration drew contorted conclusions but never revealed the details.

"The Clinton administration got these lowest possible costs by taking every assumption that would bias them down," he said. "But they were very clear about what the assumptions were. Anybody who wanted to could wade through them."

TILTING THE DISCUSSION

Some of the loudest criticisms of the administration on climate science have centered on changes to reports and other government documents dealing with the causes and consequences of global warming.

Political appointees have regularly revised news releases on climate from the National Oceanic and Atmospheric Administration, or

NOAA, altering headlines and opening paragraphs to play down the continuing global warming trend.

The changes are often subtle, but they consistently shift the meaning of statements away from a sense that things are growing warmer in unusual ways.

The pattern has appeared in reports from other agencies as well.

Several sets of drafts and final press releases from NOAA on temperature trends were provided to The Times by government employees who said they were dismayed by the practice.

On Aug. 14, 2003, a news release summarizing July temperature patterns began as a draft with this headline: "NOAA reports record and near-record July heat in the West, cooler than average in the East, global temperature much warmer than average."

When it emerged from NOAA headquarters, it read: "NOAA reports cooler, wetter than average in the East, hot in the West."

Such efforts have continued in recent weeks. Scientists at the Goddard Institute for Space Studies, a leading research center studying climate, worked with public affairs officials last month to finish a release on new studies explaining why Antarctica had experienced cooling while most of the rest of the world had warmed.

The results, just published in a refereed scientific journal, showed that the depletion of the ozone layer over Antarctica had temporarily shifted atmospheric conditions in a way that cooled the region, but that as the layer heals in coming decades, Antarctica would quickly warm.

The headline initially approved by the agency's public affairs office and the scientists was "Cool Antarctica May Warm Rapidly This Century, Study Finds."

The version that finally emerged on Oct. 6 after review by political appointees was titled "Study Shows Potential for Antarctic Climate Change."

More significant than such changes has been the scope and depth of involvement by administration appointees in controlling information flowing through the farthest reaches of government on issues that could undermine policies.

Jeffrey Ruch, who runs Public Employees for Environmental Responsibility, a network for whistle-blowers who identify government actions that violate environmental laws or rules, said the Bush administration had taken information control to a level far beyond that of its predecessor.

"The Clinton administration was less organized and systematic, with lots of infighting, kind of like the old Will Rogers joke 'I belong to no organized political party; I'm a Democrat,'" Mr. Ruch said.

"This group, for good or ill, is much more centralized," he added. "It's very controlled in the sense that almost no decision, even personnel decisions, can be made without clearance from the top. In the realm of science that becomes problematic, because science isn't neat like that."

Dr. Marburger, the president's science adviser, defended such changes.

"This administration clearly has an attitude about climate change and climate science, and it's much more cautious than the previous administration," Dr. Marburger said. "This administration also tries to be consistent in its messages. It's an inevitable consequence that you're going to get this kind of tuning up of language."

CHOOSING ADVISERS

Another area where the issue of scientific distortion keeps surfacing is in the composition of advisory panels. In a host of instances documented in news reports and by groups like the Union of Concerned Scientists, candidates have been asked about their politics. In March 2003, the American Association for the Advancement of Science criticized those queries, saying in a statement that the practice "compromises the integrity of the process of receiving advice and is inappropriate." Despite three years of charges that it is remaking scientific and medical advisory panels to favor the goals of industry or social conservatives, the White House has continued to ask some panel nominees not only about their political views, but explicitly whether they support Mr. Bush.

One recent candidate was Prof. Sharon L. Smith, an expert on Arctic marine ecology at the University of Miami.

On March 12, she received a call from the White House. She had been nominated to take a seat about to open up on the Arctic Research Commission, a panel of presidential appointees that helps shape research on issues in the far north, including the debate over oil exploration in the Arctic National Wildlife Refuge.

The woman calling from the White House office of presidential personnel complimented her résumé, Dr. Smith recalled, then asked the first and — as it turned out — only question: "Do you support the president?"

"I was taking notes," Dr. Smith recalled. "I'm thinking I've lost my mind. I was in total shock. I'd never been asked that before."

She responded she was not a fan of Mr. Bush's economic and foreign policies. "That was the end of the interview," she said. "I was removed from consideration instantly."

In interviews, senior administration officials said that most advisory panels reflected a broad array of opinions and backgrounds and that Mr. Bush had the right at least to know where candidates stood on his policies.

"The people who end up on these panels tend to be pretty diverse and clearly don't all support the president's policies," Dr. Marburger said. "I think you'd have to say that the question is not a litmus-test question. It's perfectly acceptable for the president to know if someone he's appointing to one of his advisory committees supports his policies or not."

INEVITABLE TENSION

To some extent, the war between science and the administration is a culture clash, both supporters and critics of Mr. Bush say.

"He uses a Sharpie pen," said John L. Howard Jr., a former adviser to Mr. Bush on the environment in both the White House and the Texas statehouse. "He's not a pencil with an eraser kind of guy."

In the campaign, Mr. Bush's team has portrayed this trait as an asset. His critics in the sciences say it is a dangerous liability.

Dr. Marburger argues that when scientific information is flowing through government agencies, the executive branch has every right to sift for inconsistencies and adjust the tone to suit its policies, as long as the result remains factual.

He said the recent ferment, including the attacks from the Union of Concerned Scientists, Democrats and environmental groups, all proved that the system works and that objective scientific information ultimately comes to the surface.

"I think people overestimate the power of government to affect science," he said. "Science has so many self-correcting aspects that I'm not really worried about these things."

He acknowledged that environmental and medical issues, in particular, would continue to have a difficult time in the policy arena, because the science was fundamentally more murky than in, say, physics or chemistry.

"I'm a physicist," Dr. Marburger said. "I know what you have to do to design an experiment where you get an unambiguous result. There is nothing like that in health and environment."

The situation is not likely to get better any time soon, say a host of experts, in part because of the growing array of issues either underlaid by science, like global warming, or created by science, like genetic engineering and cloning.

"Since the Sputnik era we have not seen science and technology so squarely in the center of the radar screen for people in either the executive branch or Congress," said Charles M. Vest, the president of the Massachusetts Institute of Technology and a member of the President's Council of Advisers on Science and Technology. "I think it's inevitable we're going to have increasing conflicts and arguments about the role it plays in policy."

Warning of Calamities and Hoping for a Change in 'An Inconvenient Truth'

BY A. O. SCOTT | MAY 24, 2006

CANNES, FRANCE, MAY 23 — "An Inconvenient Truth," Davis Guggenheim's new documentary about the dangers of climate change, is a film that should never have been made. It is, after all, the job of political leaders and policymakers to protect against possible future calamities, to respond to the findings of science and to persuade the public that action must be taken to protect the common interest.

But when this does not happen — and it is hardly a partisan statement to observe that, in the case of global warming, it hasn't — others must take up the responsibility: filmmakers, activists, scientists, even retired politicians. That "An Inconvenient Truth" should not have to exist is a reason to be grateful that it does.

Appearances to the contrary, Mr. Guggenheim's movie is not really about Al Gore. It consists mainly of a multimedia presentation on climate change that Mr. Gore has given many times over the last few years, interspersed with interviews and Mr. Gore's voice-over reflections on his life in and out of politics. His presence is, in some ways, a distraction, since it guarantees that "An Inconvenient Truth" will become fodder for the cynical, ideologically facile sniping that often passes for political discourse these days. But really, the idea that worrying about the effect of carbon-dioxide emissions on the world's climate makes you some kind of liberal kook is as tired as the image of Mr. Gore as a stiff, humorless speaker, someone to make fun of rather than take seriously.

In any case, Mr. Gore has long since proven to be a deft self-satirist. (He recently told a moderator at a Cannes Film Festival news conference to address him as "your Adequacy.") He makes a few jokes to leaven the grim gist of "An Inconvenient Truth," and some of them are funny, in the style of a college lecturer's attempts to keep the attention of his captive audience. Indeed, his onstage manner — pacing back and forth, fiddling with gadgets, gesturing for emphasis — is more a professor's than a politician's. If he were not the man who, in his own formulation "used to be the next president of the United States of America," he might have settled down to tenure and a Volvo (or maybe a Prius) in some leafy academic grove.

But as I said, the movie is not about him. He is, rather, the surprisingly engaging vehicle for some very disturbing information. His explanations of complex environmental phenomena — the jet stream has always been a particularly tough one for me to grasp — are clear, and while some of the visual aids are a little corny, most of the images are stark, illuminating and powerful.

I can't think of another movie in which the display of a graph elicited gasps of horror, but when the red lines showing the increasing rates of carbon-dioxide emissions and the corresponding rise in temperatures come on screen, the effect is jolting and chilling. Photographs of receding ice fields and glaciers — consequences of climate change that have already taken place — are as disturbing as speculative maps of submerged coastlines. The news of increased hurricane activity and warming oceans is all the more alarming for being delivered in Mr. Gore's matter-of-fact, scholarly tone.

He speaks of the need to reduce carbon-dioxide emissions as a "moral imperative," and most people who see this movie will do so out of a sense of duty, which seems to me entirely appropriate. Luckily, it happens to be a well-made documentary, edited crisply enough to keep it from feeling like 90 minutes of C-Span and shaped to give Mr. Gore's argument a real sense of drama. As unsettling as it can be, it is also intellectually exhilarating, and, like any good piece of pedagogy, whets the appetite for further study. This is not everything you need to know about global warming: that's the point. But it is a good place to start, and to continue, a process of education that could hardly be more urgent. "An Inconvenient Truth" is a necessary film.

Talks Begin on New International Climate Treaty

BY THOMAS FULLER | APRIL 1, 2008

BANGKOK — Representatives of more than 160 countries began formal negotiations here on Monday on a treaty to address climate change, with the secretary general of the United Nations, Ban Ki-moon, urging governments to help in "saving the planet."

The weeklong meeting will lay out the agenda for the talks, which are scheduled to conclude at the end of 2009. A rancorous meeting three months ago in Indonesia exposed deep fissures over how countries plan to approach global warming.

"Saving our planet requires you to be ambitious in what you aim, and, equally, in how hard you work to reach your goal," Mr. Ban told delegates in a recorded video message.

One of the main challenges for negotiators over the next 21 months will be reintroducing the United States to a global system of emissions reductions. The United States signed but never ratified the Kyoto Protocol, the 1997 agreement that binds wealthy countries to make specific cuts in greenhouse gases. The new treaty would follow the Kyoto Protocol after its binding terms expire in 2012.

Angela Anderson, director of the global warming program at the Pew Charitable Trusts, the American philanthropy, said negotiators were watching the United States election campaign closely for signs of increased willingness to grapple with climate change.

"We have three presidential candidates, all of whom have said they will re-engage in climate negotiations," Ms. Anderson said. "There will definitely be a new voice in the U.S."

The November presidential election will come roughly halfway through the negotiations, and many here believe negotiators will defer tough decisions until a new president is inaugurated.

The American public also appears more aware of the issue of global warming than at the start of the Bush administration.

Former Vice President Al Gore, who won a Nobel Peace Prize for his environmental advocacy, is starting a $300 million campaign this week to encourage Americans to push for aggressive reductions in greenhouse emissions.

Some countries disagree over what role wealthy and poor countries should play in reducing emissions. And even among wealthy countries there is significant discordance.

Last week, the Japanese vice trade minister, Takao Kitabata, said the method used to measure reductions in greenhouse gases in the Kyoto Protocol was "extremely unfair."

The Kyoto agreement uses 1990 as a reference point for greenhouse gas levels, mandating that industrialized countries as a group cut their emissions by at least 5 percent below 1990 levels by 2012. Japan proposed using 2005 as a new reference point, a change that would put other countries at a severe disadvantage, among them Germany. For Germany 1990 is an ideal starting point because western Germany absorbed and cleaned up the heavily polluting eastern Germany in the 1990s, allowing for a marked reduction in emissions over all.

Countries also disagree on how much to compensate developing countries for their efforts in reducing global warming. The agreement reached on the resort island Bali in December called for wealthier countries to help finance cleaner-burning energy technologies and non-fossil-fuel alternatives in developing countries. The United Nations calculates that at least $200 billion will be needed by 2030 for these changes. As a measure of the enormous potential shortfall, the world's wealthiest country, the United States, has so far proposed to contribute $2 billion over two years.

Years Later, Climatologist Renews His Call for Action

BY ANDREW C. REVKIN | JUNE 23, 2008

TWENTY YEARS AGO Monday, James E. Hansen, a climate scientist at NASA, shook Washington and the world by telling a sweating crowd at a Senate hearing during a stifling heat wave that he was "99 percent" certain that humans were already warming the climate.

"The greenhouse effect has been detected, and it is changing our climate now," Dr. Hansen said then, referring to a recent string of warm years and the accumulating blanket of heat-trapping carbon dioxide and other gases emitted mainly by burning fossil fuels and forests.

To many observers of environmental history, that was the first time global warming moved from being a looming issue to breaking news. Dr. Hansen's statement helped propel the first pushes for legislation and an international treaty to cut emissions of greenhouse gases. A treaty was enacted and an addendum, the Kyoto Protocol, was added.

Even as the scientific picture of a human-heated world has solidified, emissions of the gases continue to rise.

On Monday, Dr. Hansen, 67, plans to give a briefing organized by a House committee and say that it is almost, but not quite, too late to start defusing what he calls the "global warming time bomb." He will offer a plan for cuts in emissions and also a warning about the risks of further inaction.

"If we don't begin to reduce greenhouse gas emissions in the next several years, and really on a very different course, then we are in trouble," Dr. Hansen said Friday at NASA's Goddard Institute for Space Studies in New York, which he has directed since 1981. "Then the ice sheets are in trouble. Many species on the planet are in trouble."

In his testimony, Dr. Hansen said, he will say that the next president faces a unique opportunity to galvanize the country around the need for a transformed, nonpolluting energy system. The hearing is before the House Select Committee on Energy Independence and Global Warming.

Dr. Hansen said the natural skepticism and debates embedded in the scientific process had distracted the public from the confidence experts have in a future with centuries of changing climate patterns and higher sea levels under rising carbon dioxide concentrations. The confusion has been amplified by industries that extract or rely on fossil fuels, he said, and this has given cover to politicians who rely on contributions from such industries.

Dr. Hansen said the United States must begin a sustained effort to exploit new energy sources and phase out unfettered burning of finite fossil fuels, starting with a moratorium on the construction of coal-burning power plants if they lack systems for capturing and burying carbon dioxide. Such systems exist but have not been tested at anywhere near the scale required to blunt emissions. Ultimately he is seeking a worldwide end to emissions from coal burning by 2030.

Another vital component, Dr. Hansen said, is a nationwide grid for distributing and storing electricity in ways that could accommodate large-scale use of renewable, but intermittent, energy sources like wind turbines and solar-powered generators.

The transformation would require new technology as well as new policies, particularly legislation promoting investments and practices that steadily reduce emissions.

Such an enterprise would be on the scale of past ambitious national initiatives, Dr. Hansen said, like the construction of the federal highway system and the Apollo space program.

Dr. Hansen disagrees with supporters of "cap and trade" bills to cut greenhouse emissions, like the one that foundered in the Senate this month. He supports a "tax and dividend" approach that would raise the cost of fuels contributing to greenhouse emissions but return the revenue directly to consumers to shield them from higher energy prices.

As was the case in 1988, Dr. Hansen's peers in climatology, while concerned about the risks posed by unabated emissions, have mixed views on the probity of a scientist's advocating a menu of policy choices outside his field.

Some also do not see such high risks of imminent climatic calamity, particularly disagreeing with Dr. Hansen's projection that sea levels could rise a couple of yards or more in this century if emissions continue unabated.

Dr. Hansen is a favorite target of conservative commentators; on FoxNews.com, one called him "alarmist in chief." But many climate experts say Dr. Hansen, despite some faults, has been an essential prodder of the public and scientific conscience.

Jerry Mahlman, who recently retired from a long career in climatology, said he disagreed with some of Dr. Hansen's characterizations of the climate problem and his ideas about solutions. "On the whole, though, he's been helpful," Dr. Mahlman said. "He pushes the edge, but most of the time it's pedagogically sound."

Dr. Hansen said he was making a new public push now because the coming year presented a unique opportunity, with a new administration and the world waiting for the United States to re-engage in treaty talks scheduled to culminate with a new climate pact at the end of 2009.

He said a recent focus on China, which has surpassed the United States in annual carbon dioxide emissions, obscured the fact that the United States, Britain and Germany are most responsible for the accumulation of greenhouse gases.

Dr. Hansen said he had no regrets about stepping into the realm of policy, despite much criticism.

"I only regret that we haven't gotten the story across as well as it needs to be," he said. "And I think we're running out of time."

CHAPTER 6

The Consequences: 2010 and Beyond

Nearly every nation in the world pledged to reduce carbon emissions in the 2015 Paris Climate Accord. But President Donald J. Trump pulled the United States out of the agreement in 2018. Carbon emissions regulations were repealed. However, cities, states, and companies emerged as leaders in the fight against global warming. People faced hunger, drought, heat waves, and floods as the effects of global warming settled in.

Nations Approve Landmark Climate Accord in Paris

BY CORAL DAVENPORT | DEC. 12, 2015

LE BOURGET, FRANCE — With the sudden bang of a gavel Saturday night, representatives of 195 nations reached a landmark accord that will, for the first time, commit nearly every country to lowering planet-warming greenhouse gas emissions to help stave off the most drastic effects of climate change.

The deal, which was met with an eruption of cheers and ovations from thousands of delegates gathered from around the world, represents a historic breakthrough on an issue that has foiled decades of international efforts to address climate change.

Traditionally, such pacts have required developed economies like the United States to take action to lower greenhouse gas emissions,

President Obama delivers a statement on the climate agreement from the Cabinet Room of the White House, Dec. 12, 2015.

but they have exempted developing countries like China and India from such obligations.

The accord, which United Nations diplomats have been working toward for nine years, changes that dynamic by requiring action in some form from every country, rich or poor.

"This is truly a historic moment," the United Nations secretary general, Ban Ki-moon, said in an interview. "For the first time, we have a truly universal agreement on climate change, one of the most crucial problems on earth."

President Obama, who regards tackling climate change as a central element of his legacy, spoke of the deal in a televised address from the White House. "This agreement sends a powerful signal that the world is fully committed to a low-carbon future," he said. "We've shown that the world has both the will and the ability to take on this challenge." Scientists and leaders said the talks here represented the world's last, best hope of striking a deal that would begin to avert the most devastating effects of a warming planet.

Mr. Ban said there was "no Plan B" if the deal fell apart. The Eiffel Tower was illuminated with that phrase Friday night.

The new deal will not, on its own, solve global warming. At best, scientists who have analyzed it say, it will cut global greenhouse gas emissions by about half enough as is necessary to stave off an increase in atmospheric temperatures of 2 degrees Celsius or 3.6 degrees Fahrenheit. That is the point at which, scientific studies have concluded, the world will be locked into a future of devastating consequences, including rising sea levels, severe droughts and flooding, widespread food and water shortages and more destructive storms.

But the Paris deal could represent the moment at which, because of a shift in global economic policy, the inexorable rise in planet-warming carbon emissions that started during the Industrial Revolution began to level out and eventually decline.

At the same time, the deal could be viewed as a signal to global financial and energy markets, triggering a fundamental shift away from investment in coal, oil and gas as primary energy sources toward zero-carbon energy sources like wind, solar and nuclear power.

"The world finally has a framework for cooperating on climate change that's suited to the task," said Michael Levi, an expert on energy and climate change policy at the Council on Foreign Relations. "Whether or not this becomes a true turning point for the world, though, depends critically on how seriously countries follow through."

Just five years ago, such a deal seemed politically impossible. A similar 2009 climate change summit meeting in Copenhagen collapsed in acrimonious failure after countries could not unite around a deal.

Unlike in Copenhagen, Foreign Minister Laurent Fabius of France said on Saturday, the stars for this assembly were aligned.

The changes that led to the Paris accord came about through a mix of factors, particularly major shifts in the domestic politics and bilateral relationships of China and the United States, the world's two largest greenhouse gas polluters.

Since the Copenhagen deal collapsed, scientific studies have confirmed that the earliest impacts of climate change have started to sweep across the planet. While scientists once warned that climate change was a problem for future generations, recent scientific reports have concluded that it has started to wreak havoc now, from flooding in Miami to droughts and water shortages in China.

In a remarkable shift from their previous standoffs over the issue, senior officials from both the United States and China praised the Paris accord on Saturday night.

Secretary of State John Kerry, who has spent the past year negotiating behind the scenes with his Chinese and Indian counterparts in order to help broker the deal, said, "The world has come together around an agreement that will empower us to chart a new path for our planet."

Xie Zhenhua, the senior Chinese climate change negotiator, said, "The agreement is not perfect, and there are some areas in need of improvement." But he added, "This does not prevent us from marching forward with this historic step." Mr. Xie called the deal "fair and just, comprehensive and balanced, highly ambitious, enduring and effective."

Negotiators from many countries have said that a crucial moment in the path to the Paris accord came last year in the United States, when Mr. Obama enacted the nation's first climate change policy — a set of stringent new Environmental Protection Agency regulations designed to slash greenhouse gas pollution from the nation's coal-fired power plants. Meanwhile, in China, the growing internal criticism over air pollution from coal-fired power plants led President Xi Jinping to pursue domestic policies to cut coal use.

In November 2014 in Beijing, Mr. Obama and Mr. Xi announced that they would jointly pursue plans to cut domestic greenhouse gas emissions. That breakthrough announcement was seen as paving the way to the Paris deal, in which nearly all the world's nations have jointly announced similar plans.

The final language did not fully satisfy everyone. Representatives of some developing nations expressed consternation. Poorer countries had pushed for a legally binding provision requiring that rich countries appropriate a minimum of at least $100 billion a year to help them mitigate and adapt to the ravages of climate change. In the final deal, that $100 billion figure appears only in a preamble, not in the legally binding portion of the agreement.

"We've always said that it was important that the $100 billion was anchored in the agreement," said Tosi Mpanu-Mpanu, a negotiator for the Democratic Republic of Congo and the incoming leader of a coalition known as the Least Developed Countries coalition. In the end, though, they let it go.

Despite the historic nature of the Paris climate accord, its success still depends heavily on two factors outside the parameter of the deal: global peer pressure and the actions of future governments.

The core of the Paris deal is a requirement that every nation take part. Ahead of the Paris talks, governments of 186 nations put forth public plans detailing how they would cut carbon emissions through 2025 or 2030.

Those plans alone, once enacted, will cut emissions by half the levels required to stave off the worst effects of global warming. The national plans vary vastly in scope and ambition — while every country is required to put forward a plan, there is no legal requirement dictating how, or how much, countries should cut emissions.

Thus, the Paris pact has built in a series of legally binding requirements that countries ratchet up the stringency of their climate change policies in the future. Countries will be required to reconvene every five years, starting in 2020, with updated plans that would tighten their emissions cuts.

Countries will also be legally required to reconvene every five years starting in 2023 to publicly report on how they are doing in cutting emissions compared to their plans. They will be legally required to monitor and report on their emissions levels and reductions, using a universal accounting system.

That hybrid legal structure was explicitly designed in response to the political reality in the United States. A deal that would have assigned legal requirements for countries to cut emissions at specific levels would need to go before the United States Senate for ratification. That language would have been dead on arrival in the Republican-controlled Senate, where many members question the established science of human-caused climate change, and still more wish to thwart Mr. Obama's climate change agenda.

So the individual countries' plans are voluntary, but the legal requirements that they publicly monitor, verify and report what they are doing, as well as publicly put forth updated plans, are designed to create a "name-and-shame" system of global peer pressure, in hopes that countries will not want to be seen as international laggards.

That system depends heavily on the views of the future world leaders who will carry out those policies. In the United States, every Republican candidate running for president in 2016 has publicly questioned or denied the science of climate change, and has voiced opposition to Mr. Obama's climate change policies.

In the Senate, Mitch McConnell, the Republican leader, who has led the charge against Mr. Obama's climate change agenda, said, "Before his international partners pop the champagne, they should remember that this is an unattainable deal based on a domestic energy plan that is likely illegal, that half the states have sued to halt, and that Congress has already voted to reject."

There were few of those concerns at the makeshift negotiations center here in this suburb north of Paris. The delegates rose to their feet in applause to thank the French delegation, which drew on the finest elements of the country's longstanding traditions of diplomacy to broker a deal that was acceptable to all sides.

France's European partners recalled the coordinated Nov. 13 terrorist attacks in Paris, which killed 130 people and threatened to cast a shadow over the negotiations. But, bound by a collective good will toward France, countries redoubled their efforts.

"This demonstrates the strength of the French nation and makes us Europeans all proud of the French nation," said Miguel Arias Cañete, the European Union's commissioner for energy and climate action.

Yet amid the spirit of success that dominated the final hours of the negotiations, Mr. Arias Cañete reminded delegates that the accord was the beginning of the real work. "Today, we celebrate," he said. "Tomorrow, we have to act. This is what the world expects of us."

Scientists, Feeling Under Siege, March Against Trump Policies

BY NICHOLAS ST. FLEUR | APRIL 22, 2017

WASHINGTON — Thousands of scientists and their supporters, feeling increasingly threatened by the policies of President Trump, gathered Saturday in Washington under rainy skies for what they called the March for Science, abandoning a tradition of keeping the sciences out of politics and calling on the public to stand up for scientific enterprise.

As the marchers trekked shoulder-to-shoulder toward the Capitol, the street echoed with their calls: "Save the E.P.A." and "Save the N.I.H." as well as their chants celebrating science, "Who run the world? Nerds," and "If you like beer, thank yeast and scientists!" Some carried signs that showed rising oceans and polar bears in peril and faces of famous scientists like Mae Jemison, Rosalind Franklin and Marie Curie, and others touted a checklist of the diseases Americans no longer get thanks to vaccines.

Although drizzle may have washed away the words on some signs, they aimed to deliver the message that science needs the public's support.

"Science is a very human thing," said Ashlea Morgan, a doctoral student in neurobiology at Columbia University. "The march is allowing the public to know that this is what science is, and it's letting our legislators know that science is vitally important."

The demonstration in Washington — which started with teach-ins and a rally that packed the National Mall — was echoed by protests in hundreds of cities across the United States and around the world, including marches in Europe and Asia.

The March for Science evolved from a social media campaign into an effort to get people onto the streets.

Its organizers were motivated by Mr. Trump, who as a presidential candidate disparaged climate change as a hoax and cast suspicions on the safety of vaccines.

People gather at the Washington Monument before marching on Constitution Avenue in the March for Science on Earth Day.

Their resolve deepened, they said, when the president appointed cabinet members who seemed hostile to the sciences. He also proposed a budget with severe cuts for agencies like the National Institutes of Health — which would lose 18 percent of their funding in his blueprint — and the Environmental Protection Agency, which faces a 31 percent budget cut and the elimination of a quarter of the agency's 15,000 employees.

While traveling by motorcade to Walter Reed National Military Medical Center on Saturday, Mr. Trump passed dozens of demonstrators from the march holding signs, including one that said, "Stop denying the earth is dying," according to a pool report. Later, the White House released a statement from Mr. Trump for Earth Day that did not mention the March for Science by name, but appeared directed at its participants. Calling science critical to economic growth and environmental protection, he said, "My administration is committed to advancing scientific research that leads to a better understanding of our environment and of environmental risks."

"As we do so, we should remember that rigorous science depends not on ideology, but on a spirit of honest inquiry and robust debate," he added.

Organizers said they hoped the day's demonstrations result in sustained, coordinated action aimed at persuading elected officials to adopt policies consistent with the scientific consensus on climate change, vaccines and other issues.

"This has been a living laboratory as scientists and science institutions are willing to take a step outside their comfort zone, outside of the labs and into the public spheres," said Beka Economopoulos, a founder of the pop-up Natural History Museum and an organizer of the march.

Mona Hanna-Attisha, a pediatrician who helped expose lead poisoning in Flint, Mich., and who spoke in Washington, called the protest the beginning of a movement to ensure that governments do not dismiss or deny science.

"If we want to prevent future Flints, we need to embrace what we've learned and how far we've come in terms of science and technology," Dr. Hanna-Attisha said in an interview.

What began as a movement by scientists for scientists has drawn in many science enthusiasts, young and old.

William Harrison, 9, from Washington, held up a waterlogged cardboard sign he drew with markers of a shark pleading with humanity to save him from global warming. He said science is important because without it, "we basically will not exist."

On the West Coast, Penelope DeVries, 69, carried a sign at the march in San Francisco that said, "Love your mother," with a blue and green Earth, the paint still wet from when she made it on her kitchen floor.

"I have three grandchildren, and I want them to have a beautiful life like I have," she said.

She was one of thousands of upbeat demonstrators who marched through the city's downtown under mild weather.

A volunteer at that march, Bryan Dunyak, 28, was motivated to help improve science outreach and improve public understanding of science.

"The vast majority of people will never have the chance to ask a scientist, 'Why do you do what you do?'" said Dr. Dunyak, who is a postdoctoral researcher in neurodegenerative disease at the University of California, San Francisco.

Fearing that Mr. Trump may undermine public support for the sciences, many scientists at the marches said they believed now was the appropriate moment to express themselves politically.

"I can't think of a time where scientists felt the enterprise of science was being threatened in the way scientists feel now," Naomi Oreskes, a professor of the history of science at Harvard University, said in an interview this week.

Dr. Oreskes said the closest parallel to Saturday's protests were the demonstrations for nuclear disarmament in the 1950s and '60s. But scientists were then marching against the use of science to build weapons of mass destruction.

Thousands converged on the Boston Common in a cold rain, and children danced to a brass band. Students from Harvard and M.I.T. marched over the bridge from Cambridge, and a contingent from Boston University chanted, "What do we want? Science! When do we want it? After peer review!"

In a city and state where many work in hospitals and biomedical firms, Mr. Trump's proposals to cut the National Institutes of Health's budget were on the minds of many marchers there.

Dr. George Q. Daley, the dean of Harvard Medical School, said in a speech that the proposed cuts would have a "cataclysmic effect" on the economy in Massachusetts.

"This is a shortsighted decision that will set the biomedical enterprise on a path toward devastation," Dr. Daley said.

Julian Arthur, a product scientist who works on antibody production, agreed.

"I feel that science funding should not be up to the whims of a frugal government," he said.

In New York, demonstrators stretched for 10 blocks along Central Park West, wedged between the park and a line of buildings on a gray and dreary day.

Underlining the connection in the minds of many marchers between the science march, Earth Day and global warming, one participant, Christine Negra, 49, a chemist who works as a consultant on climate change issues, said she would attend next week's People's Climate March, too.

"In the U.S., we're lagging in our recognition about how important climate change is," she said. "These public events are meant to shake people out of their daily lives so that people see how urgent the problem really is."

Many messages at the New York rally took on a political hue. One demonstrator carried a sign with a diagram. "Before you dismiss science, Mr. President," it said, "here is the molecular formula for hair spray." Another said, "Fund science, not walls." And along the marching route, some were heard chanting, "Hey, hey, ho, ho, Donald Trump has got to go," as they passed the Trump International Hotel and Tower at Columbus Circle.

For many marchers, especially those in the sciences who were demonstrating for the first time, political settings can be a source of discomfort. And critics of the march who are in the sciences expressed concern that such displays could be damaging.

"I worry the march would drive the wedge deeper," said Robert S. Young, a coastal geologist at Western Carolina University who wrote a New York Times Op-Ed article in January expressing misgivings about the march.

Although Dr. Young planned to support friends at a satellite demonstration, he said it would be easy for conservatives to say the march was really about supporting liberal policies.

"Going to a march is easy," he said. "Spending the next couple of years reinventing how we communicate with red-state America, that's hard."

In energy-rich Oklahoma, the home state of Scott Pruitt, the E.P.A. chief who repeatedly sued the agency when he was the state's attorney general, a crowd estimated at more than 2,000 by law enforcement officials chanted "science is real."

The demonstrators gathered on a stone plaza before the State Capitol, which is fenced and scaffolded for renovation. They marched on a route that took them around a park that includes two restored oil derricks that once pumped oil from a source beneath the Capitol.

Many at the Oklahoma City march seemed motivated by local issues. Lisa Pitts, a teacher, said she was marching because of concerns about the state's education budget and to support science education.

"We are not a poor state," she said. "We should not be 50th in everything."

But concerns about the country's direction under Mr. Trump were present there, too.

"I don't want to go back to having dirty air and water," said Rene Roy, who formerly worked for the state's environmental regulator and was concerned about Mr. Pruitt's plans for the E.P.A.

Back in Washington, Denis Hayes, who was the principal organizer of the first Earth Day in 1970, said concerns like Mr. Roy's were an important source of motivation for the science march, which was coordinated with the Earth Day Network.

"You have a clear enemy," he said. "You've got a president who along with his vice president, his cabinet and his party leadership in both houses of Congress have a strong anti-environmental agenda. He's basically trying to roll back everything that we've tried to do in the last half-century."

REPORTING WAS CONTRIBUTED BY EMILY BAUMGAERTNER FROM WASHINGTON, EMILY PALMER FROM NEW YORK, BEN FENWICK FROM OKLAHOMA CITY, JESS BIDGOOD FROM BOSTON AND STACEY SOLIE FROM SAN FRANCISCO.

The U.S. Is the Biggest Carbon Polluter in History. It Just Walked Away from the Paris Climate Deal.

BY JUSTIN GILLIS AND NADJA POPOVICH | JUNE 1, 2017

THE UNITED STATES, with its love of big cars, big houses and blasting air-conditioners, has contributed more than any other country to the atmospheric carbon dioxide that is scorching the planet.

"In cumulative terms, we certainly own this problem more than anybody else does," said David G. Victor, a longtime scholar of climate politics at the University of California, San Diego. Many argue that this obligates the United States to take ambitious action to slow global warming.

But on Thursday, President Trump announced the United States would withdraw from a 195-nation agreement on climate change reached in Paris in 2015.

The decision to walk away from the accord is a momentous setback, in practical and political terms, for the effort to address climate change.

An American exit could prompt other countries to withdraw from the pact or rethink their emissions pledges, making it much harder to achieve the agreement's already difficult goal of limiting global warming to a manageable level.

It means the United States — the country with the largest, most dynamic economy — is giving up a leadership role when it comes to finding solutions for climate change.

"It is immoral," said Mohamed Adow, who grew up herding livestock in Kenya and now works in London as a leader on climate issues for Christian Aid, a relief and development group. "The countries that have done the least to cause the problem are suffering first and worst."

Some backers of the agreement argued that the large American role in causing climate change creates an outsize responsibility to help fight it, including an obligation to send billions of dollars abroad to help people in poorer countries.

The Obama administration pledged $3 billion to an international fund meant to aid the hardest-hit countries. Only $1 billion of that had been transferred to the fund by the time President Trump took office on Jan. 20. On Thursday, he pledged to walk away from the balance of the commitment, though Congress may have the last word.

Mr. Trump argued that meeting the terms of the Paris accord would strangle the American economy and lead to major job losses. Many in the manufacturing and fossil fuel industries lobbied for the United States to leave the pact, but corporate opinion has been deeply split. Leaving the Paris deal was a central Trump campaign pledge.

While the United States is historically responsible for more emissions than any other country, it is no longer the world's largest single emitter of greenhouse gases. China surpassed the United States a decade ago, and its emissions today are about double the American figure. Some of China's emissions are from the production of goods for the United States and other rich countries.

But the United States has been burning coal, oil and natural gas far longer, and today the country, with just over 4 percent of the world's population, is responsible for almost a third of the excess carbon dioxide that is heating the planet. China is responsible for less than a sixth. The 28 countries of the European Union, taken as a group, come in just behind the United States in historical emissions.

China has four times as many people as the United States, so the Chinese still burn far less fossil fuel on average than Americans — less than half as much, in fact. The typical American also burns roughly twice as much as the average person in Europe or in Japan, and 10 times as much as the average person in India.

The Trump administration made clear months ago that it would abandon the emissions targets set by President Barack Obama, walk away from pledges of money to help poor countries battle global warming, and seek to cut research budgets aimed at finding solutions to climate change.

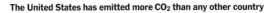

The United States has emitted more CO₂ than any other country

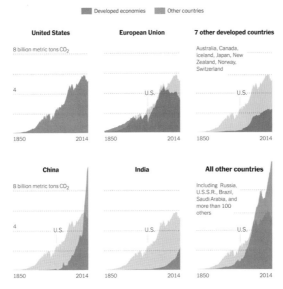

Source: Carbon Dioxide Information Analysis Center, Oak Ridge National Laboratory; country classifications via United Nations. Total CO₂ emissions are from fossil fuels and cement production and do not include land use and forestry-related emissions.

Experts say the climate crisis has become so acute that every country has to pitch in to help solve it, with no room for emissions in developing countries to reach the high levels that have been typical of rich countries.

One of the political breakthroughs that led to the Paris agreement was that nearly all the nations of the world came to grips with that reality and agreed to do what they could to help solve the problem. The agreement recognized that the poorest countries could not afford to do much on their own, which is why they were promised extensive financial and technical help.

Energy experts say that poorer countries may be able to develop their economies without depending entirely on fossil fuels, with new technologies like renewable power and electric cars plunging in cost and opening the possibility of a widespread cleanup of the world's energy system.

"Nobody really wants barrels of oil or tons of coal," said John D. Sterman, a professor of management at the Massachusetts Institute of

Technology and a founder of a think tank called Climate Interactive. "They need a warm, dry, safe place to live, and access to healthy food, and lighting when it's dark."

If it turns out that those goods can really be provided with clean energy, that may be the economic opportunity of the 21st century — and increasingly, countries like China and India seem to see things that way. Recent analyses by Climate Action Tracker, an alliance of European think tanks, suggest that both countries are on track to beat the targets they set in the Paris agreement, even as the United States backs away.

The New York Times asked Climate Interactive to calculate when Americans would have run out of fossil fuel if the nation's population had somehow, at the beginning of the industrial era, been allocated a share equal to those of the rest of the world's people. The calculation was premised on limiting emissions enough to meet international climate goals.

The answer: Americans would have used up their quota in 1944, the year the Allied armies stormed the beaches of Normandy.

Bucking Trump, These Cities, States and Companies Commit to Paris Accord

BY HIROKO TABUCHI AND HENRY FOUNTAIN | JUNE 1, 2017

REPRESENTATIVES of American cities, states and companies are preparing to submit a plan to the United Nations pledging to meet the United States' greenhouse gas emissions targets under the Paris climate accord, despite President Trump's decision to withdraw from the agreement.

The unnamed group — which, so far, includes 30 mayors, three governors, more than 80 university presidents and more than 100 businesses — is negotiating with the United Nations to have its submission accepted alongside contributions to the Paris climate deal by other nations.

"We're going to do everything America would have done if it had stayed committed," Michael Bloomberg, the former New York City mayor who is coordinating the effort, said in an interview.

By redoubling their climate efforts, he said, cities, states and corporations could achieve, or even surpass, the pledge of the administration of former President Barack Obama to reduce America's planet-warming greenhouse gas emissions 26 percent by 2025, from their levels in 2005.

It was unclear how, exactly, that submission to the United Nations would take place. Christiana Figueres, a former top United Nations climate official, said there was currently no formal mechanism for entities that were not countries to be full parties to the Paris accord.

Ms. Figueres, who described the Trump administration's decision to withdraw as a "vacuous political melodrama," said the American government was required to continue reporting its emissions to the

United Nations because a formal withdrawal would not take place for several years.

But Ms. Figueres, the executive secretary of the United Nations Framework Convention on Climate Change until last year, said the Bloomberg group's submission could be included in future reports the United Nations compiled on the progress made by the signatories of the Paris deal.

There are 195 countries committed to reducing their greenhouse gas emissions as part of the 2015 agreement.

Still, producing what Mr. Bloomberg described as a "parallel" pledge would indicate that leadership in the fight against climate change in the United States had shifted from the federal government to lower levels of government, academia and industry.

Mr. Bloomberg, a United Nations envoy on climate, is a political independent who has been among the critics of Mr. Trump's climate and energy policies.

Mayors of cities including Los Angeles, Atlanta and Salt Lake City have signed on — along with Pittsburgh, which Mr. Trump mentioned in his speech announcing the withdrawal — as have Hewlett-Packard, Mars and dozens of other companies.

Eighty-two presidents and chancellors of universities including Emory & Henry College, Brandeis and Wesleyan are also participating, the organizers said.

Mr. Trump's plan to pull out of the Paris agreement was motivating more local and state governments, as well as businesses, to commit to the climate change fight, said Robert C. Orr, one of the architects of the 2015 Paris agreement as the United Nations secretary-general's lead climate adviser.

On Thursday, Gov. Jay Inslee of Washington, Gov. Andrew M. Cuomo of New York and Gov. Jerry Brown of California, all Democrats, said they were beginning a separate alliance of states committed to upholding the Paris accord.

"The electric jolt of the last 48 hours is accelerating this process that was already underway," said Mr. Orr, who is now dean of the School of Public Policy at the University of Maryland. "It's not just the volume of actors that is increasing, it's that they are starting to coordinate in a much more integral way."

The United States is about halfway to its 2025 emissions reduction target, Mr. Orr said. Of the remaining reductions, the federal government — through regulations like gas mileage standards for vehicles — could affect about half.

But in a draft letter to António Guterres, the United Nations secretary-general, Mr. Bloomberg expressed confidence that "non-national actors" could achieve the 2025 goal alone.

"While the executive branch of the U.S. government speaks on behalf of our nation in matters of foreign affairs, it does not determine many aspects of whether and how the United States takes action on climate change," he wrote.

"The bulk of the decisions which drive U.S. climate action in the aggregate are made by cities, states, businesses, and civil society," he wrote. "Collectively, these actors remain committed to the Paris accord."

Cities and states can reduce emissions in many ways, including negotiating contracts with local utilities to supply greater amounts of renewable energy, building rapid transit programs and other infrastructure projects like improved wastewater treatment. Similarly, corporations can take measures like buying renewable energy for their offices and factories, or making sure their supply chains are climate-friendly.

Governor Inslee said that states held significant sway over emissions. Washington, for example, has adopted a cap on carbon pollution, has invested in growing clean energy jobs and subsidizes electric vehicle purchases and charging stations.

"Our states will move forward, even if the president wants to go backward," he said in a telephone interview.

America's biggest corporations have been bracing for the United

States to exit from the Paris climate accord, a move executives and analysts say would bring few tangible benefits to businesses — but plenty of backlash.

Multinational companies will still need to follow ever-stricter emissions laws that other countries are adopting, no matter the location of their headquarters. Automakers like Ford Motor and General Motors would still need to build cars that meet stringent fuel economy and emissions standards in the European Union, Japan and even China, not to mention California.

American companies also face the wrath of overseas consumers for abandoning what has been a popular global agreement — customers who could buy more Renaults instead of Chevrolets or Reeboks instead of Nikes.

"Pulling out of Paris would be the worst thing for brand America since Abu Ghraib," said Nigel Purvis, a top environmental negotiator in the Clinton and George W. Bush administrations and the chief executive of Climate Advisers, a consulting firm.

"Mars stands by the Paris Climate Agreement," said Grant Reid, the chief executive of Mars. The company, best known for its candies, remained committed, he said, to achieving "the carbon reduction targets the planet needs."

It was unclear from Mr. Trump's announcement what commitments the United States would honor in the Paris accord, which include contributions to the operating budget of the accord's coordinating agency, the framework convention.

But Bloomberg Philanthropies, Mr. Bloomberg's charitable organization, is offering to donate $14 million over the next two years to help fund the budget should it be needed, a spokeswoman said. That figure represents the United States' share, she said.

Jackie Biskupski, the mayor of Salt Lake City and a Democrat, said her administration had recently brokered an agreement with the local utility to power the city with 100 percent renewable energy by 2032.

Global warming is having a significant impact in Utah, she said, especially on water availability and quality. "We feel very strongly that we have an obligation to make sure we keep moving in the right direction on this issue," she said.

"We really have to make choices that reflect our long-term goals, that really address long-term issues of today," she added.

How G.O.P. Leaders Came to View Climate Change as Fake Science

BY CORAL DAVENPORT AND ERIC LIPTON | JUNE 3, 2017

WASHINGTON — The campaign ad appeared during the presidential contest of 2008. Rapid-fire images of belching smokestacks and melting ice sheets were followed by a soothing narrator who praised a candidate who had stood up to President George W. Bush and "sounded the alarm on global warming."

It was not made for a Democrat, but for Senator John McCain, who had just secured the Republican nomination.

It is difficult to reconcile the Republican Party of 2008 with the party of 2017, whose leader, President Trump, has called global warming a hoax, reversed environmental policies that Mr. McCain advocated on his run for the White House, and this past week announced that he would take the nation out of the Paris climate accord, which was to bind the globe in an effort to halt the planet's warming.

The Republican Party's fast journey from debating how to combat human-caused climate change to arguing that it does not exist is a story of big political money, Democratic hubris in the Obama years and a partisan chasm that grew over nine years like a crack in the Antarctic shelf, favoring extreme positions and uncompromising rhetoric over cooperation and conciliation.

"Most Republicans still do not regard climate change as a hoax," said Whit Ayres, a Republican strategist who worked for Senator Marco Rubio's presidential campaign. "But the entire climate change debate has now been caught up in the broader polarization of American politics."

"In some ways," he added, "it's become yet another of the long list of litmus test issues that determine whether or not you're a good Republican."

Since Mr. McCain ran for president on climate credentials that were stronger than his opponent Barack Obama's, the scientific evidence linking greenhouse gases from fossil fuels to the dangerous warming of the planet has grown stronger. Scientists have for the first time drawn concrete links between the planet's warming atmosphere and changes that affect Americans' daily lives and pocketbooks, from tidal flooding in Miami to prolonged water shortages in the Southwest to decreasing snow cover at ski resorts.

That scientific consensus was enough to pull virtually all of the major nations along. Conservative-leaning governments in Britain, France, Germany and Japan all signed on to successive climate change agreements.

Yet when Mr. Trump pulled the United States from the Paris accord, the Senate majority leader, the speaker of the House and every member of the elected Republican leadership were united in their praise.

Those divisions did not happen by themselves. Republican lawmakers were moved along by a campaign carefully crafted by fossil fuel industry players, most notably Charles D. and David H. Koch, the Kansas-based billionaires who run a chain of refineries (which can process 600,000 barrels of crude oil per day) as well as a subsidiary that owns or operates 4,000 miles of pipelines that move crude oil.

Government rules intended to slow climate change are "making people's lives worse rather than better," Charles Koch explained in a rare interview last year with Fortune, arguing that despite the costs, these efforts would make "very little difference in the future on what the temperature or the weather will be."

Republican leadership has also been dominated by lawmakers whose constituents were genuinely threatened by policies that would raise the cost of burning fossil fuels, especially coal. Senator Mitch McConnell of Kentucky, always sensitive to the coal fields in his state, rose through the ranks to become majority leader. Senator John Barrasso of Wyoming also climbed into leadership, then the chairmanship of the Committee on Environment and Public Works, as a champion of his coal state.

Mr. Trump has staffed his White House and cabinet with officials who have denied, or at least questioned, the existence of global warming. And he has adopted the Koch language, almost to the word. On Thursday, as Mr. Trump announced the United States' withdrawal, he at once claimed that the Paris accord would cost the nation millions of jobs and that it would do next to nothing for the climate.

Beyond the White House, Representative Lamar Smith of Texas, chairman of the House Science Committee, held a hearing this spring aimed at debunking climate science, calling the global scientific consensus "exaggerations, personal agendas and questionable predictions."

A small core of Republican lawmakers — most of whom are from swing districts and are at risk of losing their seats next year — are taking modest steps like introducing a nonbinding resolution in the House in March urging Congress to accept the risks presented by climate change.

But in Republican political circles, speaking out on the issue, let alone pushing climate policy, is politically dangerous. So for the most part, these moderate Republicans are biding their time, until it once again becomes safe for Republicans to talk more forcefully about climate change. The question is how long that will take.

"With 40 percent of Florida's population at risk from sea-level rise, my state is on the front lines of climate change," said Representative Carlos Curbelo, Republican of Florida. "South Florida residents are already beginning to feel the effects of climate change in their daily lives."

'THE TURNING POINT'

It was called the "No Climate Tax" pledge, drafted by a new group called Americans for Prosperity that was funded by the Koch brothers. Its single sentence read: "I will oppose any legislation relating to climate change that includes a net increase in government revenue." Representative Jim Jordan, Republican of Ohio, was the first member of Congress to sign it in July 2008.

AMERICANS FOR PROSPERITY

Sign the Americans for Prosperity No Climate Tax Pledge

Dear Representative,

Americans for Prosperity is launching an initiative to draw a line in the sand declaring that climate change legislation will not be used to fund a dramatic expansion in the size and scope of government. If you oppose unrestrained growth in government at taxpayers' expense and hidden under the guise of environmental political correctness, then sign the pledge at the bottom of this page and return it to our office, or visit our website at www.noclimatetax.com.

Regardless of which approach to the climate issue you favor, we should be able to agree that any climate-change policy should be revenue neutral. Revenue neutrality requires using all new revenues generated by a climate tax, cap-and-trade, or regulatory program, dollar for dollar, to cut taxes. There must also be a guarantee that climate policies remain revenue neutral over time.

The alternative to revenue-neutrality is a vast new source of federal revenue, a hidden tax that in the case of the recently debated Lieberman-Warner bill totaled $6.7 trillion over 42 years to fund a massive new shadow government.

Any major increase in federal revenue should be debated openly on its merits. We therefore encourage you to pledge to the American people that you will oppose any effort to hide a revenue increase in a feel-good environmental bill.

Sincerely,

Tim Phillips
President, Americans for Prosperity

No Climate Tax Federal Pledge:

I, Jim Jordan, pledge to the taxpayers of the state of Ohio and to the American people that I will oppose any legislation relating to climate change that includes a net increase in federal government revenue.

Signed By: _____ Date: 7/10/08
Printed Name: Tim Jordan
Witness Signature: _____
Witness Printed Name: Rory Yankura

Please Mail or Fax To:
Americans for Prosperity
1726 M Street NW
Washington, DC 20016
(202) 885-5880 - Phone
(202) 587-4599 - Fax

The "No Climate Tax" pledge signed by Representative Jim Jordan, an Ohio Republican.

The effort picked up steam the next year after the House of Representatives passed what is known as cap-and-trade legislation, a concept invented by conservative Reagan-era economists.

The idea was to create a statutory limit, or cap, on the overall amount of a certain type of pollution that could be emitted. Businesses could then buy and sell permits to pollute, choosing whether to invest more in pollution permits, or in cleaner technology that would then save them money and allow them to sell their allotted permits. The administration of the first President George Bush successfully deployed the first national cap-and-trade system in 1990 to lower emissions of the pollutants that cause acid rain. Mr. McCain pushed a cap-and-trade proposal to fight climate change.

"I thought we could get it done," recalled Henry A. Waxman, a retired House Democrat who led the cap-and-trade push in 2009. "We just had two candidates from the Republican and Democratic parties who had run for president and agreed that climate change was a real threat."

Conservative activists saw the legislative effort as an opportunity to transform the climate debate.

With the help of a small army of oil-industry-funded academics like Wei-Hock Soon of Harvard Smithsonian and think tanks like the Competitive Enterprise Institute, they had been working to discredit academics and government climate change scientists. The lawyer and conservative activist Chris Horner, whose legal clients have included the coal industry, gathered documents through the Freedom of Information Act to try to embarrass and further undermine the climate change research.

Myron Ebell, a senior fellow with the Competitive Enterprise Institute, worked behind the scenes to make sure Republican offices in Congress knew about Mr. Horner's work — although at the time, many viewed Mr. Ebell skeptically, as an extremist pushing out-of-touch views.

In 2009, hackers broke into a climate research program at the University of East Anglia in England, then released the emails that conservatives said raised doubts about the validity of the research. In one email, a scientist talked of using a statistical "trick" in a chart illustrating a recent sharp warming trend. The research was ultimately validated, but damage was done.

As Congress moved toward actually passing climate change legislation, a fringe issue had become a part of the political mainstream.

"That was the turning point," Mr. Horner said.

The House passed the cap-and-trade bill by seven votes, but it went nowhere in the Senate — Mr. Obama's first major legislative defeat.

Unshackled by the Supreme Court's Citizens United decision and other related rulings, which ended corporate campaign finance restrictions, Koch Industries and Americans for Prosperity started an all-fronts campaign with television advertising, social media and cross-country events aimed at electing lawmakers who would ensure that the fossil fuel industry would not have to worry about new pollution regulations.

Their first target: unseating Democratic lawmakers such as Representatives Rick Boucher and Tom Perriello of Virginia, who had voted for the House cap-and-trade bill, and replacing them with Republicans who were seen as more in step with struggling Appalachia, and who pledged never to push climate change measures.

But Americans for Prosperity also wanted to send a message to Republicans.

Until 2010, some Republicans ran ads in House and Senate races showing their support for green energy.

"After that, it disappeared from Republican ads," said Tim Phillips, the president of Americans for Prosperity. "Part of that was the polling, and part of it was the visceral example of what happened to their colleagues who had done that."

What happened was clear. Republicans who asserted support for climate change legislation or the seriousness of the climate threat saw their money dry up or, worse, a primary challenger arise.

"It told Republicans that we were serious," Mr. Phillips said, "that we would spend some serious money against them."

By the time Election Day 2010 arrived, 165 congressional members and candidates had signed Americans for Prosperity's "No Climate Tax" pledge.

Most were victorious.

"The midterm election was a clear rejection of policies like the cap-and-trade energy taxes that threaten our still-fragile economy," said James Valvo, then Americans for Prosperity's government affairs director, in a statement issued the day after the November 2010 election. Eighty-three of the 92 new members of Congress had signed the pledge.

Even for congressional veterans, that message was not missed. Representative Fred Upton, a Michigan Republican who once called climate change "a serious problem" and co-sponsored a bill to promote energy-efficient light bulbs, tacked right after the 2010 elections as he battled to be chairman of the powerful House Energy and Commerce Committee against Joe Barton, a Texan who mocked human-caused climate change.

Mr. Upton deleted references to climate change from his website. "If you look, the last year was the warmest year on record, the warmest decade on record. I accept that," he offered that fall. "I do not say that it's man-made."

Mr. Upton, who has received more than $2 million in campaign donations from oil and gas companies and electric utilities over the course of his career, won the chairmanship and has coasted comfortably to re-election since.

Two years later, conservative "super PACs" took aim at Senator Richard G. Lugar of Indiana, a senior Republican who publicly voiced climate concerns, backed the creation of a Midwestern cap-and-trade program and drove a Prius. After six Senate terms, Mr. Lugar lost his primary to a Tea Party challenger, Richard E. Mourdock. Although Mr. Lugar says other reasons contributed, he and his opponents say his public views on climate change played a crucial role.

"In my own campaign, there were people who felt strongly enough about my views on climate change to use it to help defeat me, and other Republicans are very sensitive to that possibility," Mr. Lugar said in an interview. "So even if they privately believe we ought to do something about it, they're reticent, especially with the Republican president taking the views he is now taking."

OBAMA FEEDS THE MOVEMENT

After winning re-election in 2012, Mr. Obama understood his second-term agenda would have to rely on executive authority, not legislation that would go nowhere in the Republican-majority Congress. And climate change was the great unfinished business of his first term.

To finish it, he would deploy a rarely used provision in the Clean Air Act of 1970, which gave the Environmental Protection Agency the authority to issue regulations on carbon dioxide.

"If Congress won't act soon to protect future generations, I will," he declared in his 2013 State of the Union address.

President Obama during his State of the Union address in the House Chamber of the Capitol, Tuesday, Feb. 12, 2013.

The result was the Clean Power Plan, which would significantly cut planet-warming emissions by forcing the closing of hundreds of heavy-polluting coal-fired power plants.

The end run around Congress had consequences of its own. To Republican (and some Democratic) critics, the Clean Power Plan exemplified everything they opposed about Mr. Obama: He seemed to them imperious, heavy-handed, pleasing to the elites on the East and West Coasts and in the capitals of Europe, but callous to the blue-collar workers of coal and oil country.

"It fed into this notion of executive overreach," said Heather Zichal, who advised Mr. Obama on climate policy. "I don't think there was a good enough job on managing the narrative."

Republicans who had supported the climate change agenda began to defect and have since stayed away.

"On the issue of climate change, I think it's happening," Mr. McCain said in a CNN podcast interview last April. But, he said, "The president decided, at least in the last couple years if not more, to rule by edict."

Mr. Obama's political opponents saw the climate rules as a ripe opportunity. "When the president went the regulatory route, it gave our side more confidence," Mr. Phillips said. "It hardened and broadened Republican opposition to this agenda."

Starting in early 2014, the opponents of the rule — including powerful lawyers and lobbyists representing many of America's largest manufacturing and industrial interests — regularly gathered in a large conference room at the national headquarters of the U.S. Chamber of Commerce, overlooking the White House. They drafted a long-game legal strategy to undermine Mr. Obama's climate regulations in a coordinated campaign that brought together 28 state attorneys general and major corporations to form an argument that they expected to eventually take to the Supreme Court.

They presented it not as an environmental fight but an economic one, against a government that was trying to vastly and illegally expand its authority.

"This is the most significant wholesale regulation of energy that the United States has ever seen, by any agency," Roger R. Martella Jr., a former E.P.A. lawyer who then represented energy companies, said at a gathering of industry advocates, making an assertion that has not been tested.

ATTORNEYS GENERAL STEP IN

Republican attorneys general gathered at the Greenbrier resort in West Virginia in August 2015 for their annual summer retreat, with some special guests: four executives from Murray Energy, one of the nation's largest coal mining companies.

Murray was struggling to avoid bankruptcy — a fate that had befallen several other coal mining companies already, given the slump in demand for their product and the rise of natural gas, solar and wind energy.

The coal industry came to discuss a new part of the campaign to reverse the country's course on climate change. Litigation was going to be needed, the industry executives and the Republican attorneys general agreed, to block the Obama administration's climate agenda — at least until a new president could be elected.

West Virginia's attorney general, Patrick Morrisey, led the session, "The Dangerous Consequences of the Clean Power Plan & Other E.P.A. Rules," which included, according to the agenda, Scott Pruitt, then the attorney general of Oklahoma; Ken Paxton, Texas' attorney general; and Geoffrey Barnes, a corporate lawyer for Murray, which had donated $250,000 to the Republican attorneys general political group.

That same day, Mr. Morrissey would step outside the hotel to announce that he and other attorneys general would sue in federal court to try to stop the Clean Power Plan, which he called "the most far-reaching energy regulation in this nation's history, drawn up by radical bureaucrats."

Mr. Pruitt quickly became a national point person for industry-backed groups and a magnet for millions of dollars of campaign contributions, as the fossil fuel lobby looked for a fresh face with conservative credentials and ties to the evangelical community.

TRUMP RULES

"Pruitt was instrumental — he and A.G. Morrisey," said Thomas Pyle, a former lobbyist for Koch Industries, an adviser to Mr. Trump's transition team and the president of a pro-fossil fuel Washington research organization, the Institute for Energy Research. "They led the charge and made it easier for other states to get involved. Some states were keeping their powder dry, but Pruitt was very out front and aggressive."

After the litigation was filed — by Mr. Morrissey and Mr. Pruitt, along with other attorneys general who attended the Greenbrier meeting — Murray Energy sued in the federal court case as well, just as had been planned.

In February 2016, the Supreme Court indicated that it would side with opponents of the rule, moving by a 5-4 vote to grant a request by the attorneys general and corporate players to block the implementation of the Clean Power Plan while the case worked its way through the federal courts.

TRUMP STOKES THE FIRES

When Donald J. Trump decided to run for president, he did not appear to have a clear understanding of the nation's climate change policies. Nor, at the start of his campaign, did he appear to have any specific plan to prioritize a huge legal push to roll those policies back.

Mr. Trump had, in 2012, said on Twitter, "The concept of global warming was created by and for the Chinese in order to make U.S. manufacturing non-competitive." But he had also, in 2009, joined dozens of other business leaders to sign a full-page ad in the The New York Times urging Mr. Obama to push a global climate change pact being negotiated in Copenhagen, and to "strengthen and pass United States legislation" to tackle climate change.

However, it did not go unnoticed that coal country was giving his presidential campaign a wildly enthusiastic embrace, as miners came out in full force for Mr. Trump, stoking his populist message.

And the surest way for Mr. Trump to win cheers from coal crowds was to aim at an easy target: Mr. Obama's climate rules. Hillary Clinton did not help her cause when she said last spring that her climate policies would "put a lot of coal miners and coal companies out of business."

In May 2016, Mr. Trump addressed one of the largest rallies of his campaign: an estimated crowd of over 10,000 in Charleston, W.Va., where the front rows were crammed with mine workers.

"I'm thinking about miners all over the country," he said, eliciting cheers. "We're going to put miners back to work."

"They didn't used to have all these rules and regulations that make it impossible to compete," he added. "We're going to take it all off the table." Then an official from the West Virginia Coal Association handed the candidate a miner's hat.

Donald Trump wears a miner's hard hat he was given on stage during his speech in front of a crowd of supporters at a campaign rally at the Charleston Civic Center in Charleston, W. Va., on May 5, 2016.

As he put it on, giving the miners a double thumbs-up, "The place just went nuts, and he loved it," recalled Barry Bennett, a former adviser to Mr. Trump's presidential campaign. "And the miners started showing up at everything. They were a beaten lot, and they saw him as a savior. So he started using the 'save coal' portions of the speech again and again."

Mr. Trump's advisers embraced the miners as emblematic of the candidate's broader populist appeal.

"The coal miners were the perfect case for what he was talking about," Mr. Bennett said, "the idea that for the government in Washington, it's all right for these people to suffer for the greater good — that federal power is more important than your little lives."

Mr. Trump took on as an informal campaign adviser Robert E. Murray — chief executive of the same coal company that had been working closely for years with the Republican attorneys general to unwind the Obama environmental legacy.

Mr. Murray, a brash and folksy populist who started working in coal mines as a teenager, is an unabashed skeptic of climate science. The coal magnate and Mr. Trump had a natural chemistry, and where Mr. Trump lacked the legal and policy background to unwind climate policy, Mr. Murray was happy to step in.

"I thank my lord, Jesus Christ, for the election of Donald Trump," Mr. Murray said soon after his new friend won the White House.

Mr. Trump appointed Mr. Ebell, the Competitive Enterprise Institute fellow who had worked for years to undermine the legitimacy of established climate science, to head the transition team at E.P.A. Mr. Ebell immediately began pushing for an agenda of gutting the Obama climate regulations and withdrawing from the Paris Agreement.

When it came time to translate Mr. Trump's campaign promises to coal country into policy, Mr. Murray and others helped choose the perfect candidate: Mr. Pruitt, the Oklahoma attorney general.

Mr. Trump, who had never met Mr. Pruitt before his election, offered him the job of E.P.A. administrator — putting him in a position to dismantle the environmental rules that he had long sought to fight in court.

Meanwhile, Mr. Trump wanted to be seen delivering on the promises he had made to the miners. As controversies piled up in his young administration, he sought comfort in the approval of his base.

In March, Mr. Trump signed an executive order directing Mr. Pruitt to begin unwinding the Clean Power Plan — and he did so at a large public ceremony at the E.P.A., flanked by coal miners and coal executives. Mr. Murray beamed in the audience.

Meanwhile, a battle raged at the White House over whether to withdraw the United States from the Paris agreement. Mr. Trump's daughter Ivanka and his secretary of state, Rex W. Tillerson, urged him to remain in, cautioning that withdrawing could be devastating to the United States' foreign policy credentials.

Murray Energy — despite its enormous clout with Mr. Trump and his top environmental official — boasts a payroll with only 6,000 employees. The coal industry nationwide is responsible for about 160,000 jobs, with just 65,000 directly in mining, according to the federal Energy Information Administration.

By comparison, General Electric alone has 104,000 employees in the United States, and Apple has 80,000. Their chief executives openly pressed Mr. Trump to stick with Paris, as did dozens of other major corporations that have continued to support regulatory efforts to combat climate change.

But these voices did not have clout in Washington, either in Congress or at the White House, when it comes to energy policy.

Mr. Trump's senior adviser, Stephen K. Bannon, backed by Mr. Pruitt, told the president that pulling out of the deal would mean a promise kept to his base.

"It is time to put Youngstown, Ohio; Detroit, Michigan; and Pittsburgh, Pennsylvania — along with many, many other locations within our great country — before Paris, France," Mr. Trump said in his Rose Garden speech on Thursday. "It is time to make America great again."

THE SCIENCE GETS STRONGER

The recognition that human activity is influencing the climate developed slowly, but a scientific consensus can be traced to a conference in southern Austria in October 1985. Among the 100 or so attendees who gathered in the city of Villach, nestled in the mountains along the Drava River, was Bert Bolin, a Swedish meteorologist and a pioneer in using computers to model the climate.

Dr. Bolin helped steer the conference to its conclusion: "It is now believed that in the first half of the next century a rise of global mean temperature could occur which is greater than any in man's history," he wrote in the conference's 500-page report.

While the politics of climate change in the United States has grown more divided since then, the scientific community has united: Global warming is having an impact, scientists say, with sea levels rising along with the extremity of weather events. Most of the debate is about the extent of those impacts — how high the seas may rise, or how intense and frequent heavy storms or heat waves may be.

In recent years, many climate scientists have also dropped their reluctance to pin significant weather events on climate change. Studies have shown that certain events — a 2015 Australian heat wave, floods in France last year and recent high temperatures in the Arctic — were made more likely because of global warming.

But in Congress, reluctance to embrace that science has had no political downsides, at least among Republicans.

"We don't yet have an example of where someone has paid a political price being on that side of it," said Michael Steel, who served as press secretary for the former House speaker John A. Boehner, the Republican presidential candidate Jeb Bush and the current House speaker, Paul D. Ryan, during his 2012 run as Mitt Romney's vice-presidential choice.

Instead, the messages of Mr. Pruitt still dominate.

"This is an historic restoration of American economic independence — one that will benefit the working class, the working poor and working people of all stripes," Mr. Pruitt said on Thursday, stepping to the Rose Garden lectern after Mr. Trump. "We owe no apologies to other nations for our environmental stewardship."

American voters — even many Republicans — recognize that climate change is starting to affect their lives. About 70 percent think global warming is happening, and about 53 percent think it is caused by human activities, according to a recent study by the Yale Program on Climate Change Communication. About 69 percent support limiting carbon dioxide emissions from coal-fired power plants.

But most public opinion polls find that voters rank the environment last or nearly last among the issues that they vote on. And views are divided based on party affiliation. In 2001, 46 percent of Democrats said they worried "a great deal" about climate change, compared with 29 percent of Republicans, according to a Gallup tracking poll on the issue. This year, concern among Democrats has reached 66 percent. Among Republicans, it has fallen, to 18 percent.

Until people vote on the issue, Republicans will find it politically safer to question climate science and policy than to alienate moneyed groups like Americans for Prosperity.

There will be exceptions. The 2014 National Climate Assessment, a report produced by 14 federal agencies, concluded that climate change is responsible for much of the flooding now plaguing many of the Miami area's coastal residents, soaking homes and disrupting businesses, and Representative Curbelo is talking about it.

"This is a local issue for me," Mr. Curbelo said. "Even conservatives in my district see the impact. It's flooding, and it's happening now."

Mr. Curbelo helped create the House Climate Solutions Caucus, 20 Republicans and 20 Democrats who say they are committed to tackling climate change.

Mr. Curbelo is confident that as the impact of climate change spreads, so will the willingness of his Republican colleagues to join him.

Outside of Congress, a small number of establishment conservatives, including a handful of leaders from the Reagan administration, have begun pushing Washington to act on climate change. Earlier this year, James A. Baker III, one of the Republican Party's more eminent senior figures, met with senior White House officials to urge them to consider incorporating a carbon tax as part of a broader tax overhaul package — a way to both pay for proposed cuts to corporate tax rates and help save the planet. A Reagan White House senior economist, Art Laffer; a former secretary of state, George P. Shultz; and Henry M. Paulson Jr., George W. Bush's final Treasury secretary, have also pushed the idea.

"There are members from deep-red districts who have approached me about figuring out how to become part of this effort," Mr. Curbelo said. "I know we have the truth on our side. So I'm confident that we'll win — eventually."

Climate Change Is Complex. We've Got Answers to Your Questions.

JUSTIN GILLIS | 2017

WE KNOW. Global warming is daunting. So here's a place to start: 17 often-asked questions with some straightforward answers.

PART 1: WHAT IS HAPPENING?

Q. *Climate change? Global warming? What do we call it?*

A. Both are accurate, but they mean different things.

You can think of global warming as one type of climate change. The broader term covers changes beyond warmer temperatures, such as shifting rainfall patterns.

President Trump has claimed that scientists stopped referring to global warming and started calling it climate change because "the weather has been so cold" in winter. But the claim is false. Scientists have used both terms for decades.

Q. *How much is the Earth heating up?*

A. Two degrees is more significant than it sounds.

As of early 2017, the Earth had warmed by roughly 2 degrees Fahrenheit (more than 1 degree Celsius) since 1880, when records began at a global scale. The number may sound low, but as an average over the surface of an entire planet, it is actually high, which explains why much of the world's land ice is starting to melt and the oceans are rising at an accelerating pace. If greenhouse gas emissions continue unchecked, scientists say, the global warming could ultimately exceed 8 degrees Fahrenheit, which would undermine the planet's capacity to support a large human population.

Q. *What is the greenhouse effect, and how does it cause global warming?*

A. We've known about it for more than a century. Really.

In the 19th century, scientists discovered that certain gases in the air trap and slow down heat that would otherwise escape to space. Carbon dioxide is a major player; without any of it in the air, the Earth would be a frozen wasteland. The first prediction that the planet would warm as humans released more of the gas was made in 1896. The gas has increased 43 percent above the pre-industrial level so far, and the Earth has warmed by roughly the amount that scientists predicted it would.

Q. *How do we know humans are responsible for the increase in carbon dioxide?*

A. This one is nailed down.

Hard evidence, including studies that use radioactivity to distinguish industrial emissions from natural emissions, shows that the extra gas is coming from human activity. Carbon dioxide levels rose and fell naturally in the long-ago past, but those changes took thousands of years. Geologists say that humans are now pumping the gas into the air much faster than nature has ever done.

Q. *Could natural factors be the cause of the warming?*

A. Nope.

In theory, they could be. If the sun were to start putting out more radiation, for instance, that would definitely warm the Earth. But scientists have looked carefully at the natural factors known to influence planetary temperature and found that they are not changing nearly enough. The warming is extremely rapid on the geologic time scale, and no other factor can explain it as well as human emissions of greenhouse gases.

Q. *Why do people deny the science of climate change?*

A. Mostly because of ideology.

Instead of negotiating over climate change policies and trying to make them more market-oriented, some political conservatives have taken the approach of blocking them by trying to undermine the science.

President Trump has sometimes claimed that scientists are engaged in a worldwide hoax to fool the public, or that global warming was invented by China to disable American industry. The climate denialists' arguments have become so strained that even oil and coal companies have distanced themselves publicly, though some still help to finance the campaigns of politicians who espouse such views.

PART 2: WHAT COULD HAPPEN?

Q. *How much trouble are we in?*

A. Big trouble.

Over the coming 25 or 30 years, scientists say, the climate is likely to gradually warm, with more extreme weather. Coral reefs and other sensitive habitats are already starting to die. Longer term, if emissions rise unchecked, scientists fear climate effects so severe that they might destabilize governments, produce waves of refugees, precipitate the sixth mass extinction of plants and animals in the Earth's history, and melt the polar ice caps, causing the seas to rise high enough to flood most of the world's coastal cities. The emissions that create those risks are happening now, raising deep moral questions for our generation.

Q. *How much should I worry about climate change affecting me directly?*

A. Are you rich enough to shield your descendants?

The simple reality is that people are already feeling the effects, whether they know it or not. Because of sea level rise, for instance, some 83,000 more residents of New York and New Jersey were flooded during Hurricane Sandy than would have been the case in a stable climate, scientists have calculated. Tens of thousands of people are already dying in heat waves made worse by global warming. The refugee flows that have destabilized politics around the world have been traced in part to climate change. Of course, as with almost all other social problems, poor people will be hit first and hardest.

Q. *How much will the seas rise?*

A. The real question is how fast.

The ocean has accelerated and is now rising at a rate of about a foot per century, forcing governments and property owners to spend tens of billions of dollars fighting coastal erosion. But if that rate continued, it would probably be manageable, experts say.

The risk is that the rate will increase still more. Scientists who study the Earth's history say waters could rise by a foot per decade in a worst-case scenario, though that looks unlikely. Many experts believe that even if emissions stopped tomorrow, 15 or 20 feet of sea level rise is already inevitable, enough to flood many cities unless trillions of dollars are spent protecting them. How long it will take is unclear. But if emissions continue apace, the ultimate rise could be 80 or 100 feet.

Q. *Is recent crazy weather tied to climate change?*

A. Some of it is.

Scientists have published strong evidence that the warming climate is making heat waves more frequent and intense. It is also causing heavier rainstorms, and coastal flooding is getting worse as the oceans rise because of human emissions. Global warming has intensified droughts in regions like the Middle East, and it may have strengthened a recent drought in California.

In many other cases, though — hurricanes, for example — the linkage to global warming for particular trends is uncertain or disputed. Scientists are gradually improving their understanding as computer analyses of the climate grow more powerful.

PART 3: WHAT CAN WE DO?

Q. *Are there any realistic solutions to the problem?*

A. Yes, but change is happening too slowly.

Society has put off action for so long that the risks are now severe, scientists say. But as long as there are still unburned fossil fuels in the ground, it is not too late to act. The warming will slow to a potentially manageable pace only when human emissions are reduced to zero. The good news is that they are now falling in many countries as a result of programs like fuel-economy standards for cars, stricter building codes and emissions limits for power plants. But experts say the energy transition needs to speed up drastically to head off the worst effects of climate change.

Q. *What is the Paris Agreement?*

A. Virtually every country agreed to limit future emissions.

The landmark deal was reached outside Paris in December 2015. The reductions are voluntary and the pledges do not do enough to head off severe effects. But the agreement is supposed to be reviewed every few years so that countries ramp up their commitments. President Trump announced in 2017 that he would pull the United States out of the deal, though that will take years, and other countries have said they would go forward regardless of American intentions.

Q. *Does clean energy help or hurt the economy?*

A. Job growth in renewable energy is strong.

The energy sources with the lowest emissions include wind turbines, solar panels, hydroelectric dams and nuclear power stations. Power plants burning natural gas also produce fewer emissions than those burning coal. Converting to these cleaner sources may be somewhat costlier in the short term, but they could ultimately pay for themselves by heading off climate damages and reducing health problems associated with dirty air. And expansion of the market is driving down the costs of renewable energy so fast that it may ultimately beat dirty energy on price alone — it already doesin some areas.

The transition to cleaner energy certainly produces losers, like coal companies, but it also creates jobs. The solar industry in the United States now employs more than twice as many people as coal mining.

Q. *What about fracking or 'clean coal'?*

A. Both could help clean up the energy system.

Hydraulic fracturing, or "fracking," is one of a set of drilling technologies that has helped produce a new abundance of natural gas in the United States and some other countries. Burning gas instead of coal in power plants reduces emissions in the short run, though gas is still a fossil fuel and will have to be phased out in the long run. The fracking itself can also create local pollution.

"Clean coal" is an approach in which the emissions from coal-burning power plants would be captured and pumped underground. It has yet to be proven to work economically, but some experts think it could eventually play a major role.

Q. *What's the latest with electric cars?*

A. Sales are still small overall, but they are rising fast.

The cars draw power at night from the electric grid and give off no pollution during the day as they move around town. They are inherently more efficient than gasoline cars and would represent an advance even if the power were generated by burning coal, but they will be far more important as the electric grid itself becomes greener through renewable power. The cars are improving so fast that some countries are already talking about banning the sale of gasoline cars after 2030.

Q. *What are carbon taxes, carbon trading and carbon offsets?*

A. It's just jargon for putting a price on pollution.

The greenhouse gases being released by human activity are often called "carbon emissions" for short. That is because two of the most important gases, carbon dioxide and methane, contain carbon. (Some other pollutants are lumped into the same category, even if they do not actually contain carbon.) When you hear about carbon taxes, carbon trading and so on, these are just shorthand descriptions of methods to put a price on emissions, which economists say is one of the most important steps society could take to limit them.

Q. *Climate change seems so overwhelming. What can I personally do about it?*

A. Start by sharing this with 50 of your friends.

Experts say the problem can only be solved by large-scale, collective action. Entire states and nations have to decide to clean up their energy systems, using every tool available and moving as quickly as they can. So the most important thing you can do is to exercise your rights as a citizen, speaking up and demanding change.

You can also take direct personal action to reduce your carbon footprint in simple ways that will save you money. You can plug leaks in your home insulation to save power, install a smart thermostat, switch to more efficient light bulbs, turn off unused lights, drive fewer miles by consolidating trips or taking public transit, waste less food, and eat less meat.

Taking one or two fewer plane rides per year can save as much in emissions as all the other actions combined. If you want to be at the cutting edge, you can look at buying an electric or hybrid car or putting solar panels on your roof. If your state has a competitive electricity market, you may be able to buy 100 percent green power.

Leading corporations, including large manufacturers like carmakers, are starting to demand clean energy for their operations. You can pay attention to company policies, support the companies taking the lead, and let the others know you expect them to do better.

These personal steps may be small in the scheme of things, but they can raise your own consciousness about the problem — and the awareness of the people around you. In fact, discussing this issue with your friends and family is one of the most meaningful things you can do.

Glossary

acid rain Rain or snow with a high concentration of acid-forming chemicals from pollutants.

biosphere The areas of Earth's surface and atmosphere where organisms live.

carbon dioxide (CO2) Gas produced by burning carbon and by exhaling. Colorless is absorbed by plants through photosynthesis.

carbon emissions Carbon dioxide put into the atmosphere by cars, airplanes or factories.

chlorofluorocarbon (CFC) Gases such as carbon, hydrogen, chlorine and fluorine used in refrigerants and aerosol propellants.

climatologist A scientist who specializes in the study of the climate, including causes and long-term effects of climate change.

combustion The process of burning something by the rapid combination of a fuel with oxygen.

ecology The branch of biology that studies the relations of organisms to each other and to their physical environment.

environmentalist A person who advocates for the protection of the environment.

fluctuation An unpredictable rise and fall in amount or number.

fossil fuel Natural fuel such as coal or gas derived from the accumulated remains of living organisms.

global warming The gradual increasing of the average temperature of Earth's atmosphere.

greenhouse effect The process by which sunlight passes through the atmosphere and generates heat, but prevents the escape of that heat, much like a greenhouse.

ice age The period during which the temperature of Earth's surface and atmosphere drop below freezing, causing the creation or expansion of glaciers.

infrared radiation The range of invisible radiation in the electromagnetic spectrum where the wavelengths are longer than visible light and shorter than radio waves.

methane The chemical compound that is the primary component of natural gas.

monsoon Heavy winds and rains in southern Asian that, during the rainy season, may cause floods.

ozone layer A layer in Earth's upper atmosphere with high ozone content that prevents most of the sun's harmful ultraviolet radiation from entering the lower atmosphere.

polemic A hostile written or verbal attack on someone or something.

Soviet Union The informal name for the Union of Soviet Socialist Republics (USSR), a nation formerly located in eastern Europe that dissolved in 1991.

third world A Cold War term referring to the developing countries of Africa, Asia and Latin America that were not aligned with the United States nor with the former USSR.

Media Literacy Terms

"Media literacy" refers to the ability to access, understand, critically assess and create media. The following terms are important components of media literacy, and they will help you critically engage with the articles in this title.

angle The aspect of a news story that a journalist focuses on and develops.

attribution The method by which a source is identified or by which facts and information are assigned to the person who provided them.

balance A principle of journalism that both perspectives of an argument should be presented in a fair way.

bias A disposition of prejudice in favor of a certain idea, person or perspective.

chronological order A method of writing a story presenting the details of the story in the order in which they occurred.

commentary A type of story that is an expression of opinion on recent events by a journalist generally known as a commentator.

credibility The quality of being trustworthy and believable, said of a journalistic source.

critical review A type of story that describes an event or work of art, such as a theater performance, film, concert, book, restaurant, radio or television program, exhibition or musical piece and offers critical assessment of its quality and reception.

editorial An article of opinion or interpretation.

fake news A fictional or made-up story presented in the style of a legitimate news story, intended to deceive readers; also commonly used as an insult to criticize legitimate news that one dislikes because of its perspective or unfavorable coverage of a subject.

feature story An article designed to entertain as well as to inform.

impartiality A principle of journalism that a story should not reflect a journalist's bias and should contain balance.

intention The motive or reason behind something, such as the publication of a news story.

inverted pyramid A method of writing a story using facts in order of importance, beginning with a lead and then gradually adding paragraphs in order of relevance from most interesting to least interesting.

motive The reason behind something, such as the publication of a news story or a source's perspective on an issue.

news story An article or style of expository writing that reports news, generally in a straightforward fashion and without editorial comment.

paraphrase The summary of an individual's words, with attribution, rather than a direct quotation of their exact words.

plagiarism An attempt to pass another person's workoff as one's own without attribution.

quotation The use of an individual's exact words indicated by the use of quotation marks and proper attribution.

reliability The quality of being dependable and accurate, said of a journalistic source.

source The origin of the information reported in journalism.

Media Literacy Questions

1. Compare the headlines of "Warming Arctic Climate Melting Glaciers Faster, Raising Ocean Level, Scientist Says" (on page 10) and "Global Warming Has Begun, Expert Tells Senate" (on page 58). Which is a more compelling headline, and why? How could the less compelling headline be changed to draw better the reader's interest?

2. "Warning of Calamities and Hoping for a Change in 'An Inconvenient Truth'" (on page 157) is an example of a critical review. What is the purpose of a critical review? Do you feel this article achieved that purpose?

3. "Years Later, Climatologist Renews His Call for Action" (on page 161) is an example of an interview. What are the benefits of providing readers with direct quotes of an interviewed subject's speech? Is the subject of an interview always a reliable source?

4. Does Andrew C. Revkin demonstrate the journalistic principle of impartiality in his article "Bush vs. the Laureates: How Science Became a Partisan Issue" (on page 147)? If so, how did he do so? If not, what could he have included to make his article more impartial?

5. Identify the various sources cited in the article "White House Admits Censoring Testimony" (on page 76). How does journalist Philip Shabecoff attribute information to each of these sources in the article? How effective are his attributions in helping the reader identify their sources?

6. What type of story is "Major 'Greenhouse' Impact is Unavoidable, Experts Say" (on page 63)? Can you identify another article in this collection that is the same type of story?

7. What is the intention of the article "Climate Change Is Complex. We've Got Answers to Your Questions." (on page 202)? How effectively does it achieve its intended purpose?

8. "The U.S. Is the Biggest Carbon Polluter in History. It Just Walked Away from the Paris Climate Deal." (on page 177) features a chart. What does this chart add to the article?

9. In "How G.O.P. Leaders Came to View Climate Change as Fake Science" (on page 186), journalists Coral Davenport and Eric Lipton directly quote Republican strategist Whit Ayres. What are the strengths of the use of a direct quote as opposed to paraphrasing? What are its weaknesses?

10. Analyze the authors' bias in "Bush's 'Whitewash Effect' on Warming" (on page 96) and "Skeptics Are Challenging Dire 'Greenhouse' Views" (on page 88). Do you think one journalist is more biased in their reporting than the other? If so, why do you think so?

11. Often, as a news story develops, journalists' approach toward the subject may change. Compare "Scientists Agree World Is Colder, But Climate Experts Meeting Here Fail to Agree on Reasons for Change" (on page 15) and "Increased Burning of Fuels Could Alter Climate" (on page 45), both by Walter Sullivan. Did new information discovered between the publication of these two articles change Walter Sullivan's perspective?

Citations

All citations in this list are formatted according to the Modern Language Association's (MLA) style guide.

BOOK CITATION

THE NEW YORK TIMES EDITORIAL STAFF. *Climate Change*. New York: New York Times Educational Publishing, 2019.

ARTICLE CITATIONS

CUSHMAN, JOHN H. "Industrial Group Plans to Battle Climate Treaty." *The New York Times*, 26 Apr. 1998, www.nytimes.com/1998/04/26/us/industrial -group-plans-to-battle-climate-treaty.html.

DAVENPORT, CORAL, AND ERIC LIPTON. "How G.O.P. Leaders Came to View Climate Change as Fake Science." *The New York Times*, 3 June 2017, www .nytimes.com/2017/06/03/us/politics/republican-leaders-climate-change.html.

DAVENPORT, CORAL. "Nations Approve Landmark Climate Accord in Paris." *The New York Times*, 12 Dec. 2015, www.nytimes.com/2015/12/13/world/ europe/climate-change-accord-paris.html.

FULLER, THOMAS. "Talks Begin on New International Climate Treaty." *The New York Times*, 1 Apr. 2008, www.nytimes.com/2008/04/01/world/asia/ 01climate.html.

GILLIS, JUSTIN. "Climate Change Is Complex. We've Got Answers to Your Questions." *The New York Times*, 19 Sept. 2017, www.nytimes.com/interactive/ 2017/climate/what-is-climate-change.html.

GILLIS, JUSTIN, AND NADJA POPOVICH. "The U.S. Is the Biggest Carbon Polluter in History. It Just Walked Away From the Paris Climate Deal." *The New York Times*, 1 June 2017, www.nytimes.com/interactive/2017/06/01/climate/ us-biggest-carbon-polluter-in-history-will-it-walk-away-from-the-paris -climate-deal.html.

GORE, AL, JR.. "To Skeptics on Global Warming…" *The New York Times*, 22 Apr. 1990, www.nytimes.com/1990/04/22/opinion/to-skeptics-on-global -warming.html.

HILL, GLADWIN. "Warming Arctic Climate Melting Glaciers Faster, Raising Ocean Level, Scientist Says." *The New York Times*, 30 May 1947, https:// www.nytimes.com/1947/05/30/archives/warming-arctic-climate-melting -glaciers-faster-raising-ocean-level.html.

KAEMPFFERT, WALDEMAR. "Warmer Climate on the Earth May Be Due To More Carbon Dioxide in the Air." *The New York Times*, 28 Oct. 1956, https:// www.nytimes.com/1956/10/28/archives/science-in-review-warmer-climate -on-the-earth-may-be-due-to-more.html.

THE NEW YORK TIMES. "Thinning Arctic Ice." 10 July 1990, www.nytimes .com/1990/07/10/science/science-watch-thinning-arctic-ice.html.

THE NEW YORK TIMES. "Warming of World's Climate Expected to Being in the '80s." *The New York Times*, 7 Jan. 1982, www.nytimes.com/1982/01/07/us/ warming-of-world-s-climate-expected-to-begin-in-the-80-s.html.

THE NEW YORK TIMES. "Worldwide Effort Is Proposed To Study Climate and Its Impact." *The New York Times*, 13 Feb. 1979, www.nytimes.com/1979/02/13/ archives/worldwide-effort-is-proposed-to-study-climate-and-its-impact.html.

REVKIN, ANDREW C. "Bush vs. the Laureates: How Science Became a Partisan Issue." *The New York Times*, 19 Oct. 2004, www.nytimes.com/2004/10/19/ science/19poli.html.

REVKIN, ANDREW C. "178 Nations Reach Climate Accord. U.S. Only Looks On." *The New York Times*, 24 July 2001, www.nytimes.com/2001/07/24/world/178 -nations-reach-a-climate-accord-us-only-looks-on.html.

REVKIN, ANDREW C. "Politics Reasserts Itself in the Debate Over Climate Change and Its Hazards." *The New York Times*, 5 Aug. 2003, www.nytimes .com/2003/08/05/science/politics-reasserts-itself-in-the-debate-over -climate-change-and-its-hazards.html.

REVKIN, ANDREW C. "A Shift in Stance on Global Warming Theory." *The New York Times*, 26 Oct. 2000, www.nytimes.com/2000/10/26/ us/a-shift-in-stance-on-global-warming-theory.html.

REVKIN, ANDREW C. "Years Later, Climatologist Renews His Call for Action." *The New York Times*, 23 June 2008, www.nytimes.com/2008/06/23/science/ earth/23climate.html.

SCHEUER, JAMES H. "Bush's 'Whitewash Effect' on Warming." *The New York Times*, 3 Mar. 1990, www.nytimes.com/1990/03/03/opinion/bush-s

-whitewash-effect-on-warming.html.

SCHMECK, HAROLD M. "Climate Changes Endanger World's Food Output." *The New York Times*, 8 Aug. 1974, www.nytimes.com/1974/08/08/archives/climate-changes-endanger-worlds-food-output-scientists-view-global.html.

SCOTT, A. O. "Warning of Calamities and Hoping for a Chance 'An Inconvenient Truth'" *The New York Times*, 24 May 2006, www.nytimes.com/2006/05/24/movies/24trut.html.

SHABECOFF, PHILIP. "Draft Report on Global Warming Foresees Environmental Havoc in U.S." *The New York Times*, 20 Oct. 1988, www.nytimes.com/1988/10/20/us/draft-report-on-global-warming-foresees-environmental-havoc-in-us.html.

SHABECOFF, PHILIP. "E.P.A. Proposes Rules To Curb Warming." *The New York Times*, 14 Mar. 1989, www.nytimes.com/1989/03/14/science/epa-proposes-rules-to-curb-warming.html.

SHABECOFF, PHILIP. "Global Warming Has Begun, Expert Tells Senate." *The New York Times*, 24 June 1988, www.nytimes.com/1988/06/24/us/global-warming-has-begun-expert-tells-senate.html.

SHABECOFF, PHILIP. "Loss of Tropical Forests Is Found Much Worse Than Was Thought." *The New York Times*, 8 June 1990, www.nytimes.com/1990/06/08/us/loss-of-tropical-forests-is-found-much-worse-than-was-thought.html.

SHABECOFF, PHILIP. "Major 'Greenhouse' Impact Is Unavoidable, Experts Say." *The New York Times*, 19 July 1988, www.nytimes.com/1988/07/19/science/major-greenhouse-impact-is-unavoidable-experts-say.html.

SHABECOFF, PHILIP. "Man Said to Tax Earth's Systems." *The New York Times*, 15 Feb. 1987, www.nytimes.com/1987/02/15/world/man-said-to-tax-earth-s-systems.html.

SHABECOFF, PHILIP. "Scholars Ask for Action Now to Save Global Environment." *The New York Times*, 6 May 1984, www.nytimes.com/1984/05/06/world/scholars-ask-for-action-now-to-save-global-environment.html.

SHABECOFF, PHILIP. "White House Admits Censoring Testimony." *The New York Times*, 9 May 1989, www.nytimes.com/1989/05/09/science/white-house-admits-censoring-testimony.html.

SIMONS, MARLISE. "Scientists Urging Gas Emission Cuts." *The New York Times*, 5 Nov. 1990, www.nytimes.com/1990/11/05/world/scientists-urging-gas-emission-cuts.html.

STEVENS, WILLIAM K. "Earlier Harm Seen in Global Warming." *The New York Times*, 17 Oct. 1990, www.nytimes.com/1990/10/17/world/earlier-harm-seen

-in-global-warming.html.

STEVENS, WILLIAM K. "Global Warming Experts Call Human Role Likely." *The New York Times*, 10 Sept. 1995, www.nytimes.com/1995/09/10/world/global -warming-experts-call-human-role-likely.html.

STEVENS, WILLIAM K. "Governments Start Preparing for Global Warming Disasters." *The New York Times*, 14 Nov. 1989, www.nytimes.com/1989/11/14/ science/governments-start-preparing-for-global-warming-disasters.html.

STEVENS, WILLIAM K. "Meeting Reaches Accord to Reduce Greenhouse Gases." *The New York Times*, 11 Dec. 1997, www.nytimes.com/1997/12/11/world/ meeting-reaches-accord-to-reduce-greenhouse-gases.html.

STEVENS, WILLIAM K. "Separate Studies Rank '90 As World's Warmest Year." *The New York Times*, 10 Jan. 1991, www.nytimes.com/1991/01/10/us/ separate-studies-rank-90-as-world-s-warmest-year.html.

STEVENS, WILLIAM K. "Skeptics Are Challenging Dire 'Greenhouse' Views." *The New York Times*, 13 Dec. 1989, www.nytimes.com/1989/12/13/us/split-forecast -dissent-global-warming-special-report-skeptics-are-challenging.html.

ST. FLEUR, NICHOLAS. "Scientists, Feeling Under Siege, March Against Trump Policies." *The New York Times*, 22 Apr. 2017, www.nytimes.com/2017/04/22/ science/march-for-science.html.

SULLIVAN, WALTER. "Increased Burning of Fuels." *The New York Times*, 20 Nov. 1979, www.nytimes.com/1979/11/20/archives/increased-burning-of-fuels -could-alter-climate-change-in-climate-is.html.

SULLIVAN, WALTER. "The Need to Work in Concert Was Clear." *The New York Times*, 18 June 1972, https://www.nytimes.com/1972/06/18/archives/the -need-to-work-in-concert-was-clear-world-conference.html.

SULLIVAN, WALTER. "Scientists Agree World Is Colder, But Climate Experts Meeting Here Fail to Agree on Reasons for Change." *The New York Times*, 30 Jan. 1961, https://www.nytimes.com/1961/01/30/archives/scientists -agree-world-is-colder-but-climate-experts-meeting-here.html.

SULLIVAN, WALTER. "Scientists Ask Why World Climate Is Changing." *The New York Times*, 21 May 1975, www.nytimes.com/1975/05/21/archives/scientists -ask-why-world-climate-is-changing-major-cooling-may-be-a.html.

SULLIVAN, WALTER. "Scientists Warn of Expected Rise Of Carbon Dioxide Content in Air." *The New York Times*, 13 Oct. 1976, www.nytimes.com/1976 /10/13/archives/scientists-warn-of-expected-rise-of-carbon-dioxide -content-in-air.html.

TABUCHI, HIROKO, AND HENRY FOUNTAIN. "Bucking Trump, These Cities, States and Companies Commit to Paris Accord." *The New York Times*, 2 June 2017, www.nytimes.com/2017/06/01/climate/american-cities-climate-standards .html.

WALD, MATTHEW L. "Pro-Coal Ad Campaign Disputes Warming Idea." *The New York Times*, 8 July 1991, www.nytimes.com/1991/07/08/business/pro -coal-ad-campaign-disputes-warming-idea.html.

Index